BETTY'S VIRGINIA CHRISTMAS

SECOND EDITION

NOW BETTY KNEW EXACTLY HOW TO DESCEND THE STAIRS INTO THE
DANCING HALL

Page 48

BETTY'S VIRGINIA CHRISTMAS

By
MOLLY ELLIOT SEAWELL

AUTHOR OF "THE SPRIGHTLY ROMANCE OF MARSAC," "PAPA BOUCHARD," "THE JUGGLERS," "LITTLE JARVIS," ETC.

WITH ILLUSTRATIONS IN COLOR BY
HENRY J. SOULEN

AND DECORATIONS BY
EDWARD STRATTON HOLLOWAY

WILDSIDE PRESS

TO BETTY RANDOL
A TALL SISTER OF THE LILIES
THIS BOOK IS INSCRIBED

CONTENTS

CHAPTER		PAGE
I.	CAPTIVATING BETTY	9
II.	A YOUNG SOLDIER	19
III.	THROUGH A DORMER WINDOW	31
IV.	KETTLE	38
V.	CHRISTMAS COMES BUT ONCE A YEAR	46
VI.	KETTLE AND OTHER THINGS	64
VII.	FORTESCUE AND ROSES AND BIRDSEYE	71
VIII.	THE SHADOW OF THE PAST	83
IX.	LOVE AND THE CHASE	89
X.	THE FLYING FEET OF THE DANCERS	96
XI.	THE DREAM OF LOVE	105
XII.	KETTLE ACTS HIS OWN ILIAD	110
XIII.	IT WAS THE SPRINGTIME	119
XIV.	PROBLEMS	130
XV.	THE BROKEN DREAM	138
XVI.	PRIDE PAYS THE PRICE	150
XVII.	THE HAND OF DESTINY	166
XVIII.	"DOAN' YOU CRY, MISS BETTY!"	173
XIX.	CALM WEATHER	179
XX.	TWILIGHT	185
XXI.	RECOMPENCE	189
XXII.	GLORIA	198
XXIII.	SUNSHINE	206

ILLUSTRATIONS

	PAGE
Now Betty Knew Exactly How to Descend the Stairs Into the Dancing Hall........*Frontispiece*	
Her Graceful Figure Making to Fortescue the Prettiest Picture He Had Ever Seen...........	87
The Scent Lay Across the Open Fields and Straggling Woodlands...............................	93
"But if You Love Me——".......................	125

CHAPTER I
CAPTIVATING BETTY

It was as cold as Christmas, and Christmas Eve it was. A thin crust of snow lay over the level landscape of lower Virginia, and the declining sun cast a lovely rose-red light upon the silver world. Afar off lay the river that led to the great bay, both river and bay frozen hard and fast as steel. The crystal air was sharp and still, and in the opaline sky a little crescent moon smiled at the sparkling stars. Along the broad lane that led from the wooded heights to the spacious brick mansion of Rosehill, seated on the river bank, a great four-horse team trotted merrily, the

BETTY'S VIRGINIA CHRISTMAS

stout farm-horses snorting with delight, and the negro driver and his helpers laughing, and singing Christmas catches, their voices echoing in the clear, cold air. The Rosehill mansion itself seemed to radiate Christmas cheer. From the warm, wide-throated chimneys curled delicate wreaths of blue smoke, and a venturesome peacock had climbed upon the flat roof and stood on one leg, warming himself comfortably against the hot chimney. The panes of the many windows glittered in the sinking sun, and on the frozen river a couple of skaters flew back and forth like birds upon the wing, their shrill little cries and laughter resounding gaily in the crisp cold.

A mile down the river lay another cheerful homestead, not stately and wide and long, with marble steps and a fine carriage drive, like Rosehill, but little and low and with a single chimney. No gorgeous peacock huddled against its one chimney, but a family of blue pigeons, finding the pigeon-cote chilly, circled about the solitary chimney, and were as merry as if they had been great splendid peacocks instead of the humble little birds that they were. The tall holly trees in all their Christmas glory of red and green, on each side of the little porch, gave the place its name of Holly Lodge. From its windows, too, streamed cheerfulness, and a golden fire sang and danced upon the broad hearth in its one small sitting-room. But Holly Lodge could not be otherwise than gay, because in it dwelt Betty Beverley, the gayest young creature alive.

Now, Betty had a splendid dowry; that is to say, she had youth, health, gaiety of heart, an indomitable spirit, and a pair of the softest, loveliest, most misleading dark eyes that were ever seen. Betty was the soul of sincerity and truth, yet she was also an arrant hypocrite and flatterer to those she loved. Likewise, she had the heart of a lion concerning burglars, tramps, runaway horses, and dangers of all sorts; but when it came to

BETTY'S VIRGINIA CHRISTMAS

caterpillars and daddy-long-legs, small spiders and frightened mice, Betty was cowardly beyond words, and shrieked and fled at the mere sight of those harmless creatures. Music and dancing were like foretastes of Heaven to Betty, who could dance twenty-five miles a night without the slightest fatigue. But she was the same gay little Betty in the long wintry days at Holly Lodge, with no one for company except her grandfather, Colonel Beverley, and his rheumatism, and Uncle Cesar and his wife, Aunt Tulip, the two old servants who had followed them into exile.

For Colonel Beverley was born and reared in the great house of Rosehill, and Betty, too, was born there, and had passed the whole of

CAPTIVATING BETTY

her short life in its stately rooms and its old walled garden, except the last year. Evil times had come upon Colonel Beverley, and the piled up mortgages at last drove him forth. The Colonel, tall and straight as an Indian, grim to look at, but gentle at heart, said truly that for himself he minded not Holly Lodge, with its few cramped rooms and its mite of a garden patch; but for little Betty—— Here, the Colonel's voice would break, and whenever this point was reached in the discussion, Betty always rushed at the Colonel and kissed him all over his handsome clear-cut, pallid face, and declared that he had insulted her by his hateful remarks, and that she would a thousand times rather live at Holly Lodge with him, than live at Rosehill with millions of dollars, without him. As Betty was very young and unsophisticated, she really believed this, and it comforted the Colonel's weary heart to hear it.

This was their first Christmas at Holly Lodge, but as Betty said to the Colonel on the afternoon of Christmas Eve:

"Granddaddy, I mean this to be the very happiest Christmas we ever had, because we are together, and your rheumatism is better, and I am going to a dance every night this week, and have a perfectly brand new white muslin gown to wear, and goodness knows

BETTY'S VIRGINIA CHRISTMAS

what will be left of it after six dances, because I never really begin to enjoy myself until I have torn my gown all to pieces!"

While Betty was saying this, she was standing, delicately poised, on a table, putting a wreath of laurel leaves around the portrait of Colonel Beverley, taken in his youth, when he was a boy officer, with his first epaulets, his hand sternly grasping his sword. Above the portrait hung the same sword, and Betty was wont to decorate the hilt with a sprig of laurel, too. The portrait was a handsome picture, and the Colonel was secretly proud of it. A part of Betty's outrageous flattery of Colonel Beverley was that to assure the Colonel, solemnly, that nothing would induce her to marry until she could find a man as handsome as he was in his youth. The Colonel, sitting in his great chair, listened to this for the hundredth time with the greatest pleasure. Since that St. Martin's summer of his youth, there had been a long period of tranquil life at Rosehill. Then had come the great tragedy of the wartime, and Colonel Beverley had put on a gray uniform, and ridden at the head of the regiment the county raised, his stalwart son, Betty's father, riding by his bridle. The Colonel came back in four years to Rosehill, but the young son lay buried on the Bed of Honor, with a bullet

CAPTIVATING BETTY

through his brave young heart. Betty was a dark-eyed baby girl in those days. Now, she was a dark-eyed girl of twenty, and was all the Colonel had left in this world. Even Rosehill went with the rest. The back of Colonel Beverley's chair was against the window which looked toward Rosehill, for the Colonel was sixty-eight, and could not forget wholly the sixty-seven years when Rosehill had been his home, and did not like to look toward the place. To make it worse, Rosehill had been bought by some rich Northern people, who had wickedly and sacrilegiously, as the Colonel considered, put a furnace in the house, electric lights and many other modern and devilish inventions, which harrowed the Colonel's soul. So, like a wise man, he turned his eyes away.

Within the plain little room were some relics that had survived the universal wreck. There was Betty's harp, to which she sang the old-fashioned ballads the Colonel loved. Then, there was the Beverley punch-bowl—a great bowl of old Lowestoft porcelain, with three medallions, representing hunting scenes, and an inscription in faded gilt, "For John Beverley, Esq., of Virginia." It had belonged to many John Beverleys, Esquires, before it came to the Colonel, and was regarded as a sort of fetich in the family.

BETTY'S VIRGINIA CHRISTMAS

Betty alone had the responsibility of dusting it, and Uncle Cesar would say solemnly:

"I'd heap ruther break my arm than break that thur bowl."

Beside the bowl, there was some quaint old silver and the 1807 decanters, huge things of pink and white cut glass, that had known good

vintages in their day. By Betty's harp lay her grandfather's fiddle case, for the Colonel loved his fiddle, and he and Uncle Cesar, his "boy," fiddled seriously together, as they had done since they were small boys together,

CAPTIVATING BETTY

sixty years before, and had got rapped over the head with the same fiddle-bow.

There were a plenty of windows in the little room, and, as muslin curtains are cheap, there were plenty of curtains, and geraniums and verbenas too were abundant, as they cost nothing at all. On the walls was a pretty paper, all roses and green leaves, pasted on by Betty's own hands, with Uncle Cesar holding the stepladder while Betty had worked, singing while she worked. It was Betty too who had painted the shabby woodwork white, daubing away gaily, and laughing at her blunders. Nevertheless, she had succeeded, for Betty was a very efficient person. The chimney had a wide throat and drew like a windlass. So, on the whole, the sitting-room at Holly Lodge was a cheerful place.

Betty, standing on a little table, was so engrossed in her occupation of getting the laurel wreath straight over the Colonel's picture, that she did not hear the tramp of a horse's hoofs outside, nor a knock at the front door, nor Uncle Cesar opening it and a man's tread in the little hall. In her eagerness, she reached up very far, and although she was a slim creature, the rickety table trembled under her light foot, and the Colonel cried out:

"Mind, Betty, mind!"

BETTY'S VIRGINIA CHRISTMAS

But it was too late. The table swayed, and Betty uttered a little shriek and came down with a crash, not upon the floor, but in the arms of a handsome young officer in his cap and military cloak, who appeared to have dropped down the chimney.

CHAPTER II

A YOUNG SOLDIER

THE Colonel started up and Uncle Cesar rushed in from the hall, followed by Aunt Tulip from the kitchen. Betty managed to disengage her skirts from the spurs of the young officer, and then stood upon her feet, utterly bewildered. The only person who was not panic-stricken was the young officer himself, who stood bowing, cap in hand.

"Pray excuse me," he said to Betty, and bowing low to her and then to the Colonel. "Just as I was about to enter the room, I saw that you were tottering, and ran forward and caught you just in time. I am afraid you would have had a bad fall, otherwise."

"You are perfectly excusable, sir," said

the Colonel, rising grandly. "Your advent was most fortunate, as, although I saw my granddaughter's danger, I had not the agility, with my years and rheumatism, to catch her as you did. May I ask to whom I am indebted?"

"I am Mr. Fortescue," said the young officer, laying a card down on the table, "of the United States Army, and the son of Mr. Fortescue of Rosehill."

Betty's quick eyes read the card as it lay on the table. "Lieutenant John Hope Fortescue, United States Army."

At that the Colonel's face changed a little. He had not yet grown used to the name of Fortescue of Rosehill. But Betty did not mind. She saw only that Mr. Fortescue was young and had a fine, supple figure and a pair of laughing eyes like her own, and a trim little black mustache and a close-cropped black head and a very graceful manner.

"I thank you, too, Mr. Fortescue," she said, holding out her slim hand, which the young lieutenant took. "I think our acquaintanceship has had a very auspicious beginning."

To this Fortescue replied gallantly:

"If it saved you from a fall, I shall certainly consider it most auspicious."

Then, they looked into each other's eyes and laughed, as young creatures do who have

A YOUNG SOLDIER

the sweet and subtle understanding of youth. The Colonel then said:

"Perhaps you know my name—Colonel Beverley—and this is my granddaughter, Miss Elizabeth Beverley. Will you be seated?"

"Grandfather only calls me Elizabeth when he is introducing me, or is very much vexed with me. On all other occasions, I am Betty," explained Betty gravely.

"Miss Betty Beverley—what a charming name!" answered Fortescue, determined to admire everything concerning this adorable Betty.

Uncle Cesar took Fortescue's military cloak away, and the young officer sat with his handsome head and elegant figure outlined against the strong light of the window.

"I must beg pardon for my intrusion," he said to the Colonel, "but I have come upon official business—hence my uniform."

"I understand, sir," replied the Colonel. "I have worn both the cadet gray and the army blue. Later, I resigned and spent some tranquil years at Rosehill. When the irrepressible conflict came, I put on a gray uniform, as did my son—my only son—the father of this young lady."

Here the Colonel indicated Betty, who spoke quickly and with pride:

BETTY'S VIRGINIA CHRISTMAS

"Yes, I am a soldier's daughter and proud of it."

"The soldier should be proud of it," promptly answered Fortescue, with a smile. Betty was no Quaker maiden, but came of fighting stock.

"My errand," continued Fortescue, turning to the Colonel, "is from my superior officer, Major Studly, who is engaged in making some military surveys in this neighborhood. We hope to go in camp by March. I have found an excellent place for our encampment, with running water for the animals, and a spring, about five miles from here, in the rolling country. I understand that the land is yours, and Major Studly asks your permission to occupy it for a month or six weeks, perhaps. Of course—er—er—compensation will be made for its use by the Government."

"Compensation be hanged!" replied the Colonel blandly. "It gives me pleasure to oblige a brother officer, although the United States Government may go to the devil!"

Fortescue smiled at this. From the great fortress forty miles away, he had made various incursions into the country, and had happened upon many gallant old irreconcilables, like Colonel Beverley, who felt it their duty to hurl defiance upon the United States Gov-

A YOUNG SOLDIER

ernment, although they were really among its best citizens.

"I thank you very much," said Fortescue, in a manner as courtly as the Colonel's, "not only for myself, but for Major Studly. We will do as little damage as possible. No doubt we shall be able to buy the wood we need for our encampment."

"Not from me, sir," promptly replied the Colonel. "You are welcome to all the wood you need, and if it is too much trouble to cut it down, burn up the fence-rails, sir."

Colonel Beverley liked to act the grand seigneur, but, owing to unfortunate circumstances, he was able to be grand only in small matters, like fence-rails.

During this conversation, Betty sat demurely in her chair. At the mention of compensation, a rosy vision passed before her eyes of a new roof to the kitchen, and possibly a new gown for herself. But when the Colonel magnanimously presented the Government of the United States with the use of his land and as many fence-rails as were necessary for fires, Betty, with a lofty spirit not unlike the Colonel's, dismissed the hope of repairing the kitchen and the dream of the new gown.

Fortescue, however, had no intention of confining his conversation to the Colonel, and so, looking toward Betty, said:

"This is my first visit to this county."

"I hope you are pleased with Rosehill," replied Colonel Beverley. "Rosehill has sheltered seven generations of Beverleys. The present mansion was built by my grandfather, succeeding a smaller house built by the first Beverley of Rosehill."

"I admire the house very much," said Fortescue. "I am only sorry that my profession will prevent me from spending much time there."

"Rosehill is a noble inheritance."

They were upon delicate ground, but it was impossible that the subject of Rosehill could be avoided at their first meeting. Fortescue congratulated himself on getting smoothly over a difficult subject.

"I hope, however," he continued, still smiling at Betty, "to make frequent visits here as long as I am stationed on this coast. I believe both the hunting and shooting are fine."

A YOUNG SOLDIER

"Excellent," said the Colonel. "It has been a good many years since I indulged in either. My granddaughter, however, likes the hunting field."

"Yes," answered Betty. "We haven't a swell hunt club like you have at the North, but our foxes are just as wary and our dogs as intelligent. Day after to-morrow there is to be the grand Christmas hunt."

"That, sir," explained Colonel Beverley, "is an annual custom in the county. The gentlemen in this vicinity all assemble at daybreak at the house of some gentleman in the neighborhood, for at daybreak the scent lies. The huntsmen have a hasty breakfast by lamp-light, and start out before sunrise. The fox is seldom caught for several hours, because we have the red fox in this county, which can double many times on his pursuers. Then the victorious huntsman presents the brush to the lady he wishes to compliment. It is a little ceremony of great antiquity. And then they have the hunt breakfast, with eggnog, the flower of all seductive beverages which bloom at Christmas time."

"Do you think it is possible," asked Fortescue of Betty, "that I, with three of my brother officers, who are spending Christmas with me, could be permitted to join in the Christmas hunt day after to-morrow?"

BETTY'S VIRGINIA CHRISTMAS

"Certainly," cried Betty. "The huntsmen are to meet at Bendover, the Carteret place, and Sally Carteret is my best friend. I'll ask Sally to invite you."

Although the great fortress lay only forty miles off, and was well known by sight to Betty Beverley and Sally Carteret and all the

other girls in the county, the dashing young officers were not much in evidence, and Betty secretly gloried at the idea of presenting four of these adorable creatures at the Christmas hunt. As for Fortescue, who knew the world well, the frank confidence and the cordial hospitality of these unsophisticated country gentlepeople delighted him beyond words.

A YOUNG SOLDIER

Then they talked awhile on what the rest of the world was talking about, Betty listening with all her ears, and putting in an occasional word. Most of Fortescue's conversation was addressed to the Colonel, but his eyes were furtively fixed on Betty's

charming face and her little feet, with buckles on her low shoes showing coquettishly from the edge of her gown. Fortescue professed an admiration and affection for Rosehill which, it must be admitted, was very much accentuated by Betty's bright eyes. Colonel Beverley, with finely shaded sarcasm, expressed regret that Fortescue's father, the great New York banker, should not spend more time at Rosehill, and Fortescue assumed an apologetic attitude for his father, and was full of regret that he himself was debarred from being much at Rosehill.

"You chose the profession of a soldier," said the Colonel, "when, as I understand, you might very well have been a well fed drone in the hive."

"Hardly," replied Fortescue, laughing. "My father doesn't like drones. He is himself a man of action and achievement, and my two brothers have been trained to work in my father's own line. But I always loved the military profession, and have no taste nor, indeed, capacity for any other. It is one of the sacrifices of an army life that I can only come to Rosehill at intervals. But wait until I retire, thirty-six years from now. Then I intend to settle myself at Rosehill permanently."

"I am afraid I can't wait so long to welcome you," said the Colonel, smiling.

"But I—can," answered Betty. "And when you come back you will find me on the retired list, too, still Miss Betty Beverley, of Holly Lodge."

Of this Fortescue expressed the utmost disbelief.

Then Fortescue and Betty talked about the

A YOUNG SOLDIER

gaieties of the Christmas week. There was to be a dance every night, in addition to the Christmas hunt. Fortescue expressed the deepest regret that, being unknown in the county, neither he nor his guests at Rosehill would be likely to receive invitations, but on this point he was reassured by Colonel Beverley.

"I understand," he said, "that you and your friends arrived only yesterday. My granddaughter told me yesterday morning that for the first time this winter smoke was coming out of the Rosehill chimneys. As soon as people find out that you are in the county, you will certainly receive invitations to everything that is desirable."

Fortescue expressed a pious hope that this might come true. Then, feeling that he had stayed as long as he possibly could for a first visit, Fortescue rose and shook hands with the Colonel, who cordially invited him and his friends to Holly Lodge. When Betty laid her little hand in his, Fortescue said, as he gave it a delicate pressure:

"If Miss Sally Carteret is kind enough to invite my friends and myself to the Christmas hunt, may I hope that you will chaperon us?"

"Yes," replied Betty; "provided you are not too lazy. On hunting mornings, I am in the saddle by six o'clock. I haven't a very imposing mount. Old Whitey pulls the rockaway, and isn't above hauling wood and going to the mill, but he has a strain of Diomede blood in him, and there's life in the old horse yet.''

This gave Fortescue an inspiration, but, being a natural diplomat, he kept it to himself.

Uncle Cesar was waiting in the narrow little passage with Fortescue's military cloak, and brought up his horse, which had been standing with the reins thrown over a limb of one of the great holly trees. As Fortescue rode past the window, sitting straight and square on his high-bred chestnut, Betty glued her nose to the window-pane, and, much to her embarrassment, was seen by Fortescue, who raised his cap, and bowed to his saddle-bow.

CHAPTER III

THROUGH A DORMER WINDOW

BETTY watched Fortescue as he galloped along the road that lay through the open fields to Rosehill. The vision of the Christmas hunt grew bright. She would see Sally Carteret that night at the dance at Marrowbone, and Sally was no more likely to deny an invitation to four captivating young officers than Betty herself. Betty brought her mind back with a jerk from this new and brilliant element which had suddenly burst into her placid life, to the preparations for Christmas. They were such as would be made in the small household of a bankrupt Virginia colonel and his granddaughter, his "boy" of sixty-five and the "boy's" wife of sixty, but they were illuminated by the true Christmas spirit, that sweet inspiration and good will, the radiance of the Star of Bethlehem. By much scheming and saving, Betty had acquired enough money to buy for the Colonel a military history in several volumes, for which he had expressed a wish. Equally, with infinite pains and secrecy, the Colonel had contrived out of his scanty purse to buy for Betty a little locket and chain; and there were simple presents for Uncle Cesar and Aunt Tulip, useful things that would make them more comfortable. And from the two old faithful servants were humble gifts that were highly rated by Betty and the Colonel. Then there were the preparations for the Christmas dinner the next day. Although there was not much money in the little brown house of Holly Lodge, there were oysters a-plenty upon the river shore, and a green turtle had been lying on his back for a week in the cellar, to be made into turtle soup for the Christmas dinner, and Aunt Tulip had a dozen bronze turkeys which kept her busy, of which the patriarch, a noble gobbler, had gobbled his last *morituri salutamus*. A dish of terrapin, and a half dozen partridges, knocked over by Uncle Cesar, who had a rusty old gun; and a

THROUGH A DORMER WINDOW

monumental plum pudding, were mere adjuncts to the feast.

It had been the Colonel's practice, at the old mansion at Rosehill, to invite half the county to his Christmas dinner. In the little sitting-room at Holly Lodge, there was not

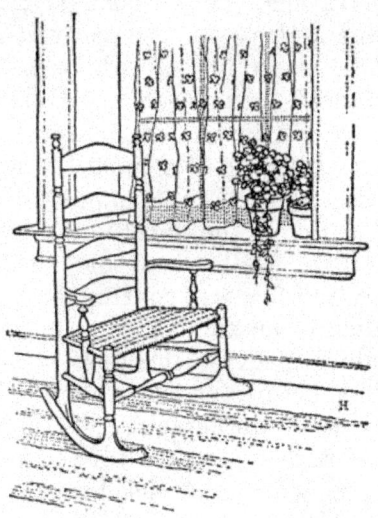

much room for anybody or anything except the big furniture and the Colonel's fiddle-case and Betty's harp; besides, the Colonel, after his misfortune, had, as yet, not much heart for company. He and Betty had had dozens of invitations from all over the county and beyond, for Christmas, but, as Betty said:

BETTY'S VIRGINIA CHRISTMAS

"Granddaddy and I have always been together at Christmas ever since I can remember, and he has nobody but me and I have nobody but him, and so we must stay together on Christmas Day, Granddaddy and I."

The dusk came before Betty had finished her preparations for the next day, and then it was time to dress for the party at Marrowbone, the Lindsay place, where there were young students home from the University of Virginia, and a great jollification was to be had. The clutch of cold upon the world had tightened as the red sun disappeared and the stars came out in the dark blue heavens. In Betty's little white bedroom, however, a glorious wood fire was roaring, and the scent of the odoriferous wood and the geraniums in the window made a delicious atmosphere. Betty stood before the fire, warming her little feet, and saying to herself:

"How I wish we could afford to have a boy to bring up wood and pick up chips and do so many things that Uncle Cesar has to do, and really isn't able, poor old soul!"

Then Betty's mind reverted to former Christmases, at Rosehill, when there were plenty of servants and plenty of everything except money, and Betty in her ignorance knew nothing of debts and duns and mortgages and such unpleasant things. She looked

THROUGH A DORMER WINDOW

about her with a little air of discontent, and thought of her beautiful big corner bed-room at Rosehill, with its marble mantel and the ornamental plaster frieze around the ceiling, and the bell to ring, by which a maid always

appeared. But, being a courageous person, Betty took herself in hand, and put an immediate stop to painful reflections. She went up to the little dressing table, lighted by a candle on each side of the mirror, and, shaking her small fist wrathfully at her reflection in the glass, proceeded to lecture herself severely.

BETTY'S VIRGINIA CHRISTMAS

"Now, Betty Beverley," she said sternly, puckering her forehead, "this sort of useless repining is perfectly disgraceful, and has got to stop. Do you understand, Betty? *It has got to stop.* You have got your grandfather and a great many comforts and blessings, and you don't owe any money, and you are young and very, very pretty——"

At this point, Betty's brow smoothed out, her eyes assumed a beatific expression, and her rosy lips came wide open, showing a lovely, elusive dimple in her left cheek.

"It is no use denying it, it is a fact and a very agreeable one, but, as Aunt Tulip says, 'Beauty ain't nothin'; behavior's all.' Your good looks won't amount to anything if you are a coward and a poltroon; and you, a soldier's daughter and granddaughter, with no more pluck than a chicken! Betty, I am ashamed of you. Now, make up your mind to act like a soldier's daughter and granddaughter——"

And at this moment, Fortescue, whose image had been lingering in Betty's memory, suddenly came to the front. She saw him in her mind's eye, galloping past the window, his military cloak around him, his cap set firmly on his handsome head, his look, his attitude, everything about him, proclaiming the soldier. Betty's smile changed from mirth

THROUGH A DORMER WINDOW

to one of dreamy anticipation. There is much flavor in the wine of life at twenty.

She went to the window, and, putting her hands on each side of her eyes, so that she could look out into the gathering gloom of the winter night, saw afar off the windows of Rosehill shining with light. On the day after Christmas she would see that young soldier again. Betty made a rapid calculation—it would be just twenty-six hours. At the thought a smile began in Betty's soft eyes and ended on her rosy lips.

CHAPTER IV
KETTLE

BEGINNING with Christmas Eve, there was a party every night for Betty, and as wind and weather count for nothing where merry young people are concerned, Betty prepared to go, in spite of the biting cold, and a knife-like wind that came howling down from Labrador. Uncle Cesar was to take her to the parties, in the little, old-fashioned rockaway, drawn by the one horse which was all the stable of Holly Lodge could boast. The homeliness of her equipage did not in the least disconcert Betty.

"Because," as Betty said to herself, "everybody knows I am Betty Beverley of Rosehill, and the Rosehill Beverleys can do as they please about carriages and clothes, and a blessed good thing it is, as the family is down on its luck at present."

KETTLE

Betty had a variety of euphemisms to disguise the unpleasant facts of life. Poverty was being down on one's luck; simple clothes were a joke; and shabbiness, a mere romantic incident, for such was the glorious philosophy of pretty Betty.

There were, however, no sighs or regrets for Betty that Christmas Eve, as she looked with shining eyes into her mirror. Her white gown, made by her own clever fingers, fitted to perfection, and revealed all the delicate loveliness of her white neck and her slender arms. Around her throat was her great-grandmother's amethyst necklace, and her simple bodice was draped with her great-grandmother's lace bertha. Her rich hair, with its soft tendrils curling upon her neck, was adorned with a wreath of ivy leaves, and tiny moss rosebuds from the rosebush in the window of the sitting-room. This little wreath gave Betty the look of a woodland nymph. Aunt Tulip, who acted as lady's maid, during the intervals of her duty as cook, housemaid, and what not, was lost in admiration, and suggested that Betty would "cert'n'y ketch a beau." This simple flattery delighted Betty, especially as all the time she was dressing her mind was fixed upon the charms of Lieutenant John Hope Fortescue of the United States Army.

BETTY'S VIRGINIA CHRISTMAS

When Betty was quite dressed, and had given herself a final survey in the glass, Aunt Tulip went down to see if the rockaway was hitched up with old Whitey. Betty, left alone, blew out the candles, and, drawing the curtains, looked out of her window once more at Rosehill, a mile across the open fields. Yes, the house was lighted up cheerfully—it was Betty's pet grievance that the place was unoccupied for such long intervals. In some way, after that visit from Jack Fortescue, Betty was more reconciled to Mr. Fortescue's owning Rosehill. She could imagine how jolly it must be there with half a dozen young officers, and if they were all as charming as Lieutenant John Hope Fortescue—— Betty blushed at the remembrance of her descent from the top of the table into Fortescue's arms.

While Betty was chasing these fancies, like white butterflies in the sun, she noticed a small black figure far down the lane. It was coming toward Holly Lodge, tramping with short steps through the crust of snow. As the object drew nearer, Betty's keen eyes discovered that it was a small boy—a very small boy. Betty wondered why so small a child should be sent out in the winter night. When he came within the circle of red light from the front door, Betty saw that the boy was black and very ragged.

KETTLE

By this, it was time for Betty to go downstairs and show herself to the adoring eyes of her grandfather. Colonel Beverley, sitting in his great chair by the fire, surveyed Betty with profound satisfaction as she marched solemnly up and down, and pirou-

etted before him to show her new white satin slippers, with glittering buckles. From the wreath of roses down to these little slippers, the Colonel found Betty altogether adorable, and told her so.

While Betty was giving stern orders to the Colonel to go to bed promptly at ten o'clock, and not to smoke more than two pipes, Aunt

BETTY'S VIRGINIA CHRISTMAS

Tulip came into the sitting-room from the nearby kitchen.

"Miss Betty," proclaimed Aunt Tulip, with the air of announcing a catastrophe, "what you think done happen now? Them good-for-nothin' niggers that come here from I dunno where, and brought a little boy wid 'em, done gone away—they tooken the boat to-day at the landin'. And this heah boy as ain't got no father nor no mother, and say he doan's believe he never had none, got skeered at the steamboat, and turn 'roun' and run away heah! What we gwine ter do 'bout him?"

"Bring him in," cried Betty, suddenly remembering the little boy she had seen creeping through the snow.

Aunt Tulip disappeared and returned with a small colored boy, very black, very ragged, almost shoeless, but with beady eyes cheerful as Betty's own, and a row of shining teeth which he showed freely. The solemn book of life evidently had no terrors for him.

As he saw Betty in her party gown, with the wreath on her delicate head, a rapturous look came into the eyes of the waif, his grin broadened, he seemed to have a vision of Paradise.

"Why," cried Betty, "he's as black as the kettle! What's your name, little boy?"

KETTLE

"Solomon 'Zekiel Timons," replied the waif, now fairly laughing with joy amid his rags.

"Where did you come from?" asked the Colonel.

Then Solomon 'Zekiel Timons, prompted by Aunt Tulip, told his story. He lived with some colored people who were always on the move. Lately, they had been living not far from Holly Lodge, and the waif knew Miss Betty by sight, and thought she was "the beautifulest lady ever I see." He did not know whether the colored people were related to him or not, nor where he was born, nor anything except his name. He had not been ill-treated, but he did not always have enough to eat, and he knew his "clo'es was mighty raggety." The colored people were going somewhere by the steamboat, and he had gone that day to the wharf with them, their belongings packed on an ox-cart. But on reaching the wharf, and seeing the steamboat, Solomon Ezekiel's heart had fainted within him. The grin left his little black face, and his round beady eyes grew terrified when he described in jerky sentences the horrors of the steamboat.

"There wuz two gre't wheels," he gasped, opening his arms wide, "as big as dis heah house—an' they keeps on a-churnin' and a-churnin'! An' a awful thing on top de boat goin' up an' down like dis"—here Solomon 'Zekiel gave a very realistic imitation of the propeller of a side-wheel steamer in motion.

"An' den"—his frightened voice sank to a whisper—"'fo' it reach de wharf, de steamboat hollered—it jes' keep on hollerin' an' screechin' an' de smoke jes' po' outen a chimley, an' de steamboat everlastin' hollerin'. An' I wuz so skeered, I jes' run offen de wharf an' come heah."

Solomon 'Zekiel coolly ignored the fact that the steamboat landing was five miles away, and that he had trudged through the biting cold and the snow, in his poor rags and broken shoes, all that distance—and he was a very little fellow indeed.

"Have you had anything to eat since breakfast?" asked Betty, with melting eyes.

"Naw, 'm," promptly answered Solomon 'Zekiel.

"And this is Christmas Eve!" cried Betty. "Now Aunt Tulip will take you into the kitchen and give you a good supper, Solomon 'Zekiel—oh, I can't stand all that name—you are as black as the kettle, so we'll just call you Kettle for the present."

His new name and the prospect of supper seemed to delight the little negro beyond words.

KETTLE

By that time Uncle Cesar had driven the rockaway up to the door, and the Colonel was handing Betty in and muffling her up, as one muffles up his chief and only treasure. Aunt Tulip brought out Uncle Cesar's fiddle-case with his fiddle, for Uncle Cesar was an essential person in that neighborhood, on account of his expert fiddling. Old Whitey, a big, handsome horse, was dancing about in a manner so sprightly, in spite of his thirteen years, that Betty felt certain he would make a good appearance at the Christmas hunt.

CHAPTER V

CHRISTMAS COMES BUT ONCE A YEAR

It was not much after seven o'clock, but early hours are kept in the country, and there was a six-mile drive between Holly Lodge and Marrowbone. Betty enjoyed the drive, inhaling the icy, crisp night air as if it were champagne. Old Whitey did the six miles in less than an hour, and Betty was in the thick of the arrivals for the party. The hospitable host, Major Lindsay—for there were many majors and colonels in Virginia in those days—met his guests on the great portico, with the big wooden Doric columns.

"How do you do, Miss Betty?" Major Lindsay said. "And where is the Colonel, pray?"

CHRISTMAS COMES BUT ONCE A YEAR

"Granddaddy sent his compliments and regrets, but he says he is really too rheumatic to go out to dances," answered Betty, slipping out of the rockaway.

"Nonsense, nonsense!" shouted the Major, who was big and florid and handsome. "The Colonel is as able to shake a leg as ever he was, by George! I hope Cesar has brought the fiddle, because we are reckoning upon him."

"Yes, sirree," answered Uncle Cesar, with important emphasis. "I got some rheumatiz, too, same like ole Marse, but mine is in my legs, thank God A'mighty, and ain't tech my bow arm yet, praise the Lamb!"

Betty tripped up the steps, and Major Lindsay gallantly escorted her into the wide hall.

Within this great hall were Christmas mirth and cheeriness, and laughter and bright eyes and gay smiles. The house, following the plan of most houses of eastern Virginia, had a splendid great hall, big enough for a ball-room, and always used for dancing; for the people of Virginia are inveterate dancers, and a house is but poorly provided which cannot furnish space for balls. Holly wreaths were everywhere, and over each door was a sprig of mistletoe, causing the ladies to scamper through the doorways with little shrieks of laughter, while the gentlemen used strategies to intercept them.

Already dancing had begun, though the orchestra was by no means complete without Uncle Cesar. But the impatient young feet could not wait. Isaac Minkins, a saddle-colored person, who combined the profession of driving a fish-cart in the day-time and fiddling in the evening, was the director of the orchestra, and his sole assistant, until Uncle Cesar arrived, was a coal black youth who also helped on the fish-cart, and who performed upon the concertina, or, as the negroes call it, the "lap organ." Uncle Cesar, who was quickly hustled into the hall, promptly tuned up and played second fiddle.

By that time Betty had run upstairs, thrown off her cloak, taken one hasty but satisfactory view of herself in the mirror, and was stepping daintily down the staircase. Now, Betty, who was a scheming and designing creature, knew exactly how to descend the stairs into the dancing hall. This descent down the fine staircase in full view of the assembled company was an effective part of the programme, and the artful Betty, with an outspread fan in one hand and holding up her filmy white skirts with the other just enough to show her little white satin slippers, was the prettiest picture imaginable. So

CHRISTMAS COMES BUT ONCE A YEAR

thought Lieutenant John Hope Fortescue of the United States Army, and several other admirers, both old and new. As Betty came down the stairs with what appeared to be un-

studied grace, but was not, her soft eyes swept the dancers below, and she nodded and smiled back at those who recognized her. But she did not see Fortescue until she was almost at the last step, when he came forward and took her hand. He had been strikingly handsome in uniform, and he was scarcely less so in his well fitting evening clothes, although his throat, I can tell you, we were so glad to accept."

"And I am *so* glad you did," said Betty affably.

She had never laid eyes on Fortescue until four hours before, but Betty was Southern, and a Virginian at that, and readily assumed a tone of the warmest friendship with every personable young man she met, immediately after making his acquaintance.

"And now," continued Betty in an imploring tone, as if there were not another man within a hundred miles, "will you be kind enough to take me up to Mrs. Lindsay to speak to her?"

"Certainly," replied Fortescue, placing her little gloved hand within his arm, and improving his opportunities as he did so.

It was not an easy matter for Betty to reach Mrs. Lindsay, standing at the other end of the hall. Betty was stopped every minute by girls speaking to her, and by young men asking dances of her. The girls called her "Betty" and the young men called her "Miss Betty," so Fortescue promptly dropped the formal "Miss Beverley" and called her "Miss Betty," as if he had known her for a hundred years.

Meanwhile, the first fiddle and the "lap organ," reinforced by Uncle Cesar's stout

BETTY'S VIRGINIA CHRISTMAS

Betty, like all women, had a secret hankering for uniforms.

"Good evening, Miss Beverley," said Fortescue, and Betty gave a pretty little start of real surprise.

"Good evening," she said, and then hesitated.

"And how did I get here?" said Fortescue, laughing and answering the look of surprised inquiry in Betty's eloquent face. "The greatest streak of luck that ever happened! When I got back to Rosehill, I found Major Lindsay had come to call—the kindest and most hospitable people that ever lived are in Virginia, I believe—and he invited us to come over to this party. We fairly jumped down

BETTY'S VIRGINIA CHRISTMAS

bow arm, were playing energetically "I'se Gwine Back to Dixie," and Betty's slender feet danced rather than walked up the hall. At last they were standing before Mrs. Lindsay, stout, handsome, and florid, like the Major, and receiving her guests with heartfelt hospitality like her husband. The hostess greeted Betty warmly, and, above the music and merry chatter, screamed without any punctuations whatever:

"How do you do Betty so glad to see you sorry your grandfather can't be here tell him to rub his knees with turpentine every night. Tom's brought four of his friends from the University and you must dance with them all so delighted to have Mr. Fortescue and the other officers from Rosehill go right into the library and get some hot biscuit and coffee you must be so cold after your drive how do you do," etc., etc., saying the same kind things to the next arrival.

CHRISTMAS COMES BUT ONCE A YEAR

And then Tom Lindsay, a University of Virginia sophomore, swooped down on Betty; but just as he caught her hand, Fortescue, who knew both how to act and to think, put his arm around Betty's waist, and they whirled off to the strains of "I'se gwine back to Dixie, where the orange-blossoms blow." Betty, however, managed to put her hand for a second in Tom Lindsay's and to say, as everybody said to everybody else:

"Oh, so glad to see you! Have just been dying of loneliness without you;" and when safely out of Tom's hearing Betty whispered into Fortescue's ear, "Such a nice boy! We used to play together. Of course, I have to say things like that to the child." By which it may be seen that Miss Betty Beverley was a most unprincipled person when it came to dealing with personable young men, and did not have the New England conscience or any other conscience, where flattering a person of the other sex was concerned.

When the dance was over, Fortescue, like an able commander, following up his advantage, mentioned to Betty that they should accept Mrs. Lindsay's suggestion and go into the library and have the coffee and biscuits which were always served immediately upon the arrival of guests at a Virginia party. This did not appeal particularly to Betty, but

BETTY'S VIRGINIA CHRISTMAS

when Tom Lindsay came up and told her that he wanted to introduce his fellow students to her, and they would all go into the library together for coffee, Fortescue suddenly remembered that he must introduce his brother officers also to Betty. This was enough to send Betty rapidly into the library, where she found herself in an Elysium of University students and second lieutenants. Being a generous soul, Betty seized upon Sally Carteret, a tall, handsome girl, and divided her plunder of students and officers with Sally. It was only necessary to mention that Mr. Fortescue and his friends would stay over Christmas day, for Sally to invite them to

the Christmas hunt and breakfast at Bendover. Seeing there was no chance of monopolizing Betty, Fortescue found Sally, with her gypsy beauty, by no means a bad substitute.

CHRISTMAS COMES BUT ONCE A YEAR

Between the dances, raids were made into the library, where from a big table hot coffee and buttered biscuits, with "old ham" that had been cured in the smoke from hickory ashes for a couple of years—a great Virginia luxury—and a round of beef, were served as a mere preliminary to the big supper which was coming later. By the great fireplace stood a table with a huge bowl of apple toddy. The older gentlemen, who were at cards in the drawing-room with prim, elderly ladies, made frequent incursions upon the apple toddy. The ladies carefully avoided this seductive brew and kept to weak tea and thin biscuit.

Over all was the true spirit of Christmas gaiety, the heart-whole and heart-given hospitality of a hospitable people.

BETTY'S VIRGINIA CHRISTMAS

The dancing went on gaily until half past eleven o'clock, when the concoction of the Christmas eggnog began. Every gentleman was supplied with a silver fork and a plate in which had been broken the whites of four eggs. They had to be beaten so stiff that the plate could be held over the head of a lady without dropping upon her. Such was the

tradition, but only a few ladies took the risk, holding out, meanwhile, their dainty handkerchiefs over their heads to catch the whipped-up whites in case they fell. Betty was one of the venturesome ones, and Fortescue was her cavalier, and turned the plate over her head, but not a drop fell upon Betty's outspread lace handkerchief. Then the whites of the eggs were mixed with the beaten up yolks and the whipped cream and the "stiffening" as Major Lindsay called it, who, as

CHRISTMAS COMES BUT ONCE A YEAR

host, did the mixing, and then ladled out the foaming eggnog. At twelve o'clock exactly Major Lindsay held up his glass and shouted, "Merry Christmas!" and a great chorus went up of "Merry Christmas! Merry, merry Christmas!" Then, Isaac Minkins, with a magnificent flourish of his bow, burst forth into the strains of "The Flowing Bowl." All joined in the great Christmas song, Major Lindsay's big baritone leading the chorus:

> "For to-night we'll merry, merry be,
> For to-night we'll merry, merry be,
> For to-night we'll merry, merry be,
> And to-morrow we'll be sober."

Then the gentlemen roared out:

> "Here's to the man who drinks good ale and goes to bed
> quite mellow.
> He lives as he ought to live, and dies a damned good fellow.
> He lives as he ought to live,
> He lives as he ought to live,
> He lives as he ought to live,
> And dies a damned good fellow.
>
> "Here's to the man who drinks no ale and goes to bed
> quite sober.
> He withers as the leaves do, and dies in the month of
> October.
> He withers as the leaves do,
> He withers as the leaves do,
> He withers as the leaves do,
> And dies in the month of October."

Then came the verse in which all the ladies joined with great enthusiasm:

BETTY'S VIRGINIA CHRISTMAS

"Here's to the girl who gets a kiss, and runs and tells her mother.
May she live to be an old maid, and never get another!"

The chorus pealed out, Betty Beverley's clear and ringing soprano above all the rest:

"May she live to be an old maid,
May she live to be an old maid,
May she live to be an old maid,
And never get another."

Then the folding doors to the dining-room were thrown open and the real supper was served, to which coffee, biscuit, "old ham," and the round of beef were merely the appetizers. An emperor of a turkey was at the head of the table, with another at the foot, and one at each side scarcely inferior in imperial splendor. There were cold pickled oysters, and hot oysters, creamed, steamed, fried, stewed, and in scallop shells. There were great dishes of terrapin, not indeed the diamond-back of Maryland fame, but the slider, a dry-land terrapin, an excellent creature when accompanied with the butter, cream, eggs, sherry, and brandy which are lavished upon him. There were, of course, more old hams, rounds of beef, and a gigantic saddle of Southdown mutton, which Major Lindsay himself carved with a magnificent flourish. The boned turkey was a gem, the

CHRISTMAS COMES BUT ONCE A YEAR

work in the case being done by Dr. Markham, the cheery, pleasant-faced village doctor, who, it was popularly reported, in getting the bones out of the turkey used the identical instruments with which he cut off legs and arms. But the doctor's services being in demand by hostesses at Christmas time, no prejudice existed against either the boned turkey or the doctor.

There were pigeon-pie, wild ducks, chicken salad, and a few other incidentals, to be topped off by ices, custards, jellies, and cakes of innumerable varieties. It took an hour to get through with the supper, and when the guests had feasted and left the dining-room, there was still enough left to feed a couple of regiments.

The musicians had had their supper and a glass of apple toddy, and eggnog in addition, and were ready again with fiddles and "lap organ" to start the flying feet once more. Betty had more partners than she could accommodate, and told each one the same story in various forms, punctuated by a sidelong glance, which was Betty's own— that she only wished she could dance with him all the evening. Tom Lindsay, a handsome youngster, who called Betty by her first name and assumed proprietary rights over her, was encouraged to do so by this arch-hypocrite of a girl. But in this Betty only followed the prevailing fashion. All of the university students and young officers present, except Fortescue, found themselves involved in at least half a dozen desperate flirtations, which promised to continue during the whole week, and then never to be heard of again.

It was four o'clock in the wintry Christmas morning before the musicians tuned up for the final Virginia reel. The two lines were formed down the great hall, and extending through the folding doors into the library. The elders sat around, the card-players in the drawing-room giving up their games of old-fashioned whist to watch the dancers. Betty Beverley had the honor of leading off with Major Lindsay, an agile and graceful dancer in spite of his two hundred pounds. Fortescue, with the eye of a strategist, took the least desirable position at the other end of the line, but by this he acquired the privilege of

CHRISTMAS COMES BUT ONCE A YEAR

meeting Betty in the middle of the line, swinging her around first by the right hand and then by the left, next by both hands and then *dos-à-dos,* and passing under the arch. The musicians played with the fire and enthusiasm peculiar to their race. The fiddlers wagged their heads, beat time with their feet, flourished their bows, while the youth with the "lap organ" stood up and fairly danced with delight as the strains of "Forked Deer" and "Billy in the Low Grounds" rent the air.

When the two ends of the reel were danced, Major Lindsay and Betty tripped down the middle, the Major cutting the pigeon-wing and taking many quaint and curious steps, which were followed by Betty's twinkling feet. Then they danced back again, and began swinging the row of dancers until they had reached the end of the line again. The march followed next, Betty leading the ladies, and the Major leading the men, all clapping time rhythmically with the dashing music. This was gone through religiously with every couple in the reel, and it took an hour to be danced. Then, at last, it finished up in the grand chain, everybody shaking hands with everybody else, and wishing each other "Merry Christmas."

It was still pitch dark in the December morning, although past five o'clock. The

BETTY'S VIRGINIA CHRISTMAS

carriages were brought up to the door, and the ladies were shot into them, the horses prancing in the freezing air and restless to take the road. Betty was one of the last to leave, as Uncle Cesar had to "wrop up" his fiddle carefully, put it in the case, and carry it tenderly out to the rockaway. Old Whitey came up to the big Doric portico, stepping high and snorting as if he were a colt. Major Lindsay escorted Betty down the steps of the great portico, but at the foot Fortescue, bareheaded in the winter darkness, was waiting. He gave Betty's slender hand one last pressure, wrapped her delicate feet up warmly in the blanket, and got a sweet parting glance from the girl's fair eyes before Uncle Cesar called out:

"Gee up, ole hoss!"

Betty leaned back in the rockaway as old Whitey trotted briskly along the frozen road. She was in one of those happy dreams that are the glorious heritage of sweet and twenty. Her mind was divided between the charms of dashing university students and charming young officers, together with speculations as to whether her white muslin gown really would last through Christmas week. There were several alarming rents in it already, for Betty had enjoyed herself very, very much.

Then her thoughts turned to soberer things,

CHRISTMAS COMES BUT ONCE A YEAR

such as the way the brave old Colonel stood the translation from Rosehill to Holly Lodge, and the necessity for making both ends meet, and the building of a stable for their one cow. For Betty's outside and inside by no means corresponded. On the outside, she was all laughter and singing and dancing, like a silver fountain in the golden sun. Inside, she was the most level-headed, the most thoughtful, and the most courageous creature in the world. Betty was practical and sentimental, tender and cruel, gay and sad, bold and timorous, and always Betty.

CHAPTER VI

KETTLE AND OTHER THINGS

MEANWHILE, things had happened at Holly Lodge. The Colonel had taken out his violin and played dreamily the old airs, von Weber's "Last Waltz," "Love Not," and "Bygone Hours." At sixty-eight, one has many Christmas days to look back upon. The faithful heart of Aunt Tulip in the kitchen was touched when the delicate strains of the violin floated upon the air.

"Ole Marse, he jes' cipherin'." Ciphering, in the negro language, means brooding with sadness and melancholy.

But then Aunt Tulip's attention was dis-

KETTLE AND OTHER THINGS

tracted by the newcomer, Kettle. The boy, huddled close to the fire, his hands locked around his knees, his shining black eyes fixed on the blaze, was filled with deep content; he was warm, he had had a good supper, and he had escaped the dangers of the screaming steamboat. Those who had left him behind had not been too kind to him, and he had no regrets for them. Suddenly his enjoyment of the *dolce far niente* was rudely interrupted by Aunt Tulip, who herself seldom indulged in the sweet-do-nothing.

"Look a-heah, boy," she said, "I'm agoin' to give you a good washin' and put you to bed. Boys oughter be abed by this time, so they k'yarn' git in no mo' mischief 'twell to-morrer mornin'."

With that Kettle was ruthlessly seized, his clothes stripped off him, and he was soused in a washtub of warm water, while Aunt Tulip, with a scrub-brush, and soft soap of her own manufacture, scrubbed him from head to foot, including his woolly head. Kettle, who had rather dreaded the unusual experience, enjoyed it before he got through. Then Aunt Tulip, putting a nightgown of her own on him, covered him up in a little pallet she had made upon the floor of her own room, next the kitchen, and in two minutes Kettle had passed into the dreamless sleep of a tired

BETTY'S VIRGINIA CHRISTMAS

little boy. Aunt Tulip began to examine the boy's worn clothes. They were very ragged, and his shoes quite beyond help. But clothes, however ragged, may be washed and mended. So Aunt Tulip, who had worked hard all that

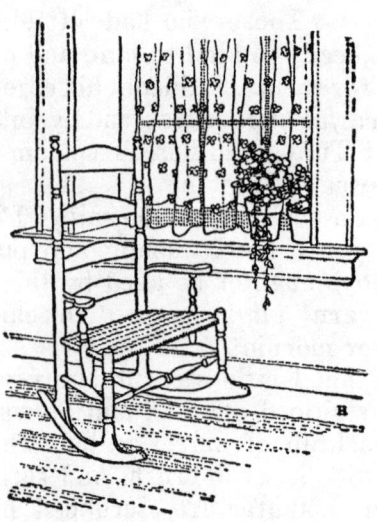

day and every day, set herself the task of having something decent for Kettle to put on Christmas morning. She toiled at the washtub while Betty, afar off, was dancing, and the Colonel had long since gone to his bedroom on the ground floor. After Kettle's poor clothes were washed and ironed, they

KETTLE AND OTHER THINGS

were hung before the kitchen fire to dry, and then Aunt Tulip, getting out her big workbasket and brass thimble and putting on her horn spectacles, began the work of mending Kettle's rags. She patched and darned industriously, and at last, with a sigh of profound satisfaction, she folded up and laid upon a chair Kettle's clothes, including his jacket and trousers, neatly washed and mended and decent. Nothing could be done with his shoes, except to put some shoe-polish on them, and this she did. The Christmas stars looked down kindly upon the poor negro woman toiling for one of God's poor, and the Christmas angels wafted a benediction upon her humble head.

When her labor was over, Aunt Tulip lay down to rest for a couple of hours. She knew well enough when Betty would return, and the fire had to be started up in Betty's room, and, after old Whitey had been put in the stable, Uncle Cesar must have his hot coffee and corn pone. For Aunt Tulip, like many of her humble sort, was a minister of kindness to all around her.

It was six o'clock, but still the world was all inky blackness when the wheels of the rockaway crunched before the door of Holly Lodge. The fire in Betty's room had been stirred into a cheering blaze, and Aunt Tulip was ready to help her out of her simple evening gown.

"I declar, Miss Betty," said Aunt Tulip, as she unhooked Betty, "how some folks kin let a chile go as raggety as that air boy, I doan' see."

Betty's mind came back from officers and university students to Kettle.

"We must try and get him some decent clothes, Mammy," answered Betty, Aunt Tulip having been Betty's mammy in her baby days.

"Anyhow," continued Aunt Tulip, "the

KETTLE AND OTHER THINGS

boy has got sumpin' decent fur Chrismus' mornin'. I done washed his clo'es an' mended 'em up the bes' I could."

"And were you washing and ironing and mending all this Christmas night?" asked Betty.

"Well," replied Aunt Tulip, "I didn't mind settin' up an' gittin' the boy's things kinder decent. But, Miss Betty, the boy has got to have a Chrismus stockin'."

"Of course," cried Betty. "You can put some apples and oranges and nuts in it."

"An' Cesar an' me kin give him a quarter apiece to'des a new pair of shoes. His shoes ain' nothin' 'tall."

Betty dived into her dressing-table drawer and took out of her little purse a dollar bill.

"And this is from Grandfather, for the shoes, too. He would never forgive us if something wasn't put into the boy's stocking from him. Now, what can I think of to give him?"

"He ain' got no collar nor cravat," said Aunt Tulip. "He would look right nice tomorrer if he jes' had a collar and cravat."

Betty was well off in collars, and produced four. Then, unfastening the scarlet ribbon from around her waist, she seized her needle and thimble, and in five minutes had sewed the ribbon into a large and very presentable cravat, and proceeded to fringe out the ends. Aunt Tulip watched her with delighted eyes.

"Lord!" she said, "that chile will be tickled to death when he gits his Chrismus' stockin'. An' you know, Miss Betty, I been thinkin' that boy could be mighty useful at Holly Lodge, pickin' up chips and carryin' the wood upstairs and huntin' up the turkeys."

"I think so, too," replied Betty, rolling up the cravat and the collars. "If he is any good, he could save you and Uncle Cesar a great many steps."

Presently, Betty was in her little white bed for a short nap, because she could not think of not being up and dressed on Christmas morning, although she had danced twenty-five miles between eight o'clock in the evening and five in the morning. Aunt Tulip, too, took what she called her "cat nap," and at eight o'clock on Christmas morning everything was awake and stirring at Holly Lodge.

CHAPTER VII

FORTESCUE AND ROSES AND BIRDSEYE

The Christmas sun was shining brilliantly, and it was not so desperately cold as the day before. Betty had hopes that the thin skim of snow would melt, so that the scent would lie for the fox-hunt the next morning. She ran downstairs as soon as she was dressed, and found the Colonel standing on the hearth-rug, his back to the fire, and his eyes turned resolutely away from Rosehill. Betty kissed him all over his face, and commanded him to be cheerful, as everybody should be on Christmas morning. Then Aunt Tulip and Uncle Cesar were called in for their simple gifts, and Kettle appeared with them, his

BETTY'S VIRGINIA CHRISTMAS

clothes clean and respectable-looking. There was much talk between the Colonel and Uncle Cesar over Christmas days long past, and the Colonel, whatever his heart might be, carried out to the letter Betty's injunction to be cheerful. As for Kettle, the sight of his Christmas stocking and his treasures, the collars and the gorgeous red cravat, and the magnificent prospect of a pair of new shoes, completely overwhelmed him. He could only look first at Betty and then at Aunt Tulip, and say to himself:

"This is the fust Chrismus I ever see; the fust Chrismus I ever see."

"Didn't you ever have a Christmas stocking before, Kettle?" asked Betty.

"Naw, Miss," answered Kettle. "I done heah 'bout 'em, but I ain't never had none befo'."

Kettle's bliss was further augmented when Aunt Tulip put a standing collar around his neck and tied the flaming red necktie under his chin. All was then swallowed up in Kettle's rapture over his own appearance. He stood before the old-fashioned mirror over the pier table, his head barely reaching the top; his mouth came open as if it were on hinges, his eyes danced in his head, and words failed him. There are moments of rapture when speech is a superfluity, and so it was

FORTESCUE AND ROSES AND BIRDSEYE

with Kettle when he beheld himself in his first cravat, and that a large one of brilliant red.

"Now, boy," said Aunt Tulip severely, who did not believe in wasting indulgences on boys, "now that Miss Betty and ole Marse done been so good to you, you got to do all you kin to holp along. You got to pick up chips an' fotch water an' black ole Marse's shoes an' do everything you know how."

"I cert'n'y will," answered Kettle fervently. And then the divine spirit of gratitude appeared in his eyes, and he said:

"An' I ain' gwine to fergit that you washed my clo'es."

"An' washed you, too," replied Aunt Tulip. "An' you got to do it yourself every day, or I'll see to you."

This awful and indefinite threat impressed Kettle with a wholesome fear of the most harmless creature on earth—Aunt Tulip.

Then breakfast was served, and Kettle received his first lessons in bringing in batter-cakes. In the intervals between the relays of hot batter-cakes, Kettle glued his eyes to his own image in the glass with a vanity second only to that of Narcissus.

Of course, the Colonel had to hear all about the party, and who was there, and if the regulation Christmas festivities were thoroughly carried out.

BETTY'S VIRGINIA CHRISTMAS

"Once," said the Colonel, "we celebrated Christmas that way at Rosehill, with an unstinted hospitality. Now——"

"Haven't I told you," cried Betty, sternly from across the table, "that you were not to make a single complaint against Fate on Christmas Day? Didn't I tell you yesterday I knew this was going to be the pleasantest Christmas I ever had? So far it certainly has been. The dance last night was the most heavenly thing—my gown is in ribbons, but I can mend it up all right, and put in a couple of new breadths later in the week. And Mr. Fortescue told me he thought that a white muslin gown at Christmas time, with scarlet ribbons and a wreath of geranium leaves, with moss rosebuds, was the most beautiful and poetic costume a girl could wear."

The Colonel's white teeth showed under his trim gray moustache.

"Fortescue knows how to pay compliments, my dear," he said.

"All right," cried Betty. "A man who doesn't know how to pay compliments and isn't equal to telling colossal fibs to the girl he is dancing with, isn't the man for me."

When breakfast was over Uncle Cesar brought in the only melancholy news of the day. Old Whitey had gone lame, and there was no going to church that day, nor was it

FORTESCUE AND ROSES AND BIRDSEYE

likely that he would be fit to ride the next day at the hunt. Betty sighed deeply. The crust of snow was rapidly disappearing, and the ground would be in good condition for the hunt. However, Betty was of a hopeful nature, and felt sure that a horse would drop down out of the clouds for her to ride.

The Christmas dinner was to be served at the old-fashioned hour of four o'clock, so when breakfast was over and Betty had paid a visit to old Whitey, she went up to her room and, throwing herself upon her bed, began to make up her lost arrears of sleep. The Colonel was downstairs absorbed in his new histories, which Betty had given him for his Christmas gift, and Betty slept peacefully until it was quite three o'clock, and the winter sun was beginning to decline. Then, as she lay awake thinking pleasant thoughts, her door was noiselessly opened, and Kettle appeared above his red cravat, carrying a big bouquet of white roses. He laid the roses down on Betty's pillow, and said:

"The gent'man who fotch 'em is downstairs—Mr. Fortescue."

Betty sat up and buried her face in the fresh roses. She knew them well. They came from the greenhouse at Rosehill, and she herself had taught them to bloom late and luxuriantly.

"Tell the gentleman I will be down immediately," she said, and then, running to her mirror, proceeded to make a fetching toilette out of very simple elements. Her well fitting dark blue gown set off her slender figure, and when she came into the sitting-room, carrying her huge bunch of roses, Fortescue, who sat talking to the Colonel, thought she looked like a peach ripening on the southern wall.

"I thank you so much," said Betty sweetly to Fortescue. "I tended the roses in the greenhouse at Rosehill as long as we lived there. We have no greenhouse here, so we couldn't bring the rose-bushes with us. But I always had roses for Christmas."

"And I hope you will always have roses for Christmas," replied Fortescue gallantly.

Then they sat and talked gaily together as young people do, of dances and hunting and

FORTESCUE AND ROSES AND BIRDSEYE

all of the great affairs of youth, the Colonel putting in a word occasionally. Fortescue was lucky enough to be asked to all the Christmas parties.

"I should like," he said, "to give a party at Rosehill, but I don't know how. I am only a man, you know. I should wish to do it right,

but I am afraid I can't make it quite as it ought to be on short notice. Now, next Christmas, if I can get leave, I will have a party, too. That is, if you, Miss Betty, will help me."

The Colonel liked the modesty of this speech, and at once said that Betty would help.

Then Betty told the melancholy story of

old Whitey's lameness. Fortunately, Sally Carteret, knowing that old Whitey had to be saved for the hunt, had invited Betty to go with her to the party that evening at Red Plains, which was close by.

"Do you mean," asked Fortescue, "that you are to miss the hunt?"

"I am afraid so," said poor Betty dolefully.

"But that isn't to be thought of," cried Fortescue. "I have several horses at Rosehill, and I can give you a mount. Birdseye, that I rode over here, is the gentlest and kindest horse that ever stepped. Although not a regular hunter, she can get along the road and over the fences all right."

"Oh!" exclaimed Betty, jumping up, "do let me see her! Granddaddy, may I ride Birdseye to-morrow morning?"

The Colonel hesitated a moment.

"I should require, my love," he said, "to

FORTESCUE AND ROSES AND BIRDSEYE

see Birdseye. Perhaps she has never had a side-saddle on her, or known what a riding-skirt is."

"We can try her," suggested Fortescue.

Betty ran out into the little hall, and, picking up a red scarf, threw it over her head, calling back to the Colonel:

"Don't you dare, Granddaddy, to come out on the porch. You can see from the window."

Fortescue was not a foot behind Betty, and they both ran to where Birdseye, dancing to keep herself warm, stood under a great holly tree. From the kitchen window peeped a little round, black face.

"We can try Birdseye with that little black boy," said Fortescue. "She wouldn't hurt a baby."

Betty beckoned to Kettle, who came out willingly enough, his constitutional grin overspreading his face.

"Run to the stable and get a horse-blanket," said Betty, which Kettle proceeded to do, and returned in a couple of minutes.

But Kettle's face suddenly changed when Fortescue, catching him by the shoulder, wrapped the horse-blanket around him as if it were a skirt, and Betty supplied a couple of hair-pins with which to fasten it. Then Fortescue, flinging the boy on Birdseye's back, put the reins in his hand, saying:

BETTY'S VIRGINIA CHRISTMAS

"Now, you little scamp, gallop around the lawn."

Kettle, his scared eyes nearly bouncing out of his little black face, his grin wholly disappeared, was quite incapable of taking a gallop around the lawn of his own initiative. He clung desperately to the reins, and began to stutter.

"G-g-g-g-ood Gord A'mighty, Miss Betty! I's jes' skeered to death of this heah hoss!"

Birdseye, however, well bred, well behaved, and intelligent, paid no attention to the squirming, frightened burden upon her shapely back. Fortescue, taking her by the bridle, led her to the paling around the little lawn, and then, with a twig broken from a big holly tree, gave her a sharp cut on the flank. Birdseye knew what was expected, and, rising, she made a beautiful standing jump over the paling. At that Kettle, with a yell, dropped the reins and grabbed the mare around the neck with both arms. Not even this could disturb Birdseye's admirable poise. Fortescue himself made a standing leap over the paling and, running Birdseye around, made her do another beautiful jump over the paling. By that time, not even fear of Fortescue or love of Betty could keep Kettle on Birdseye's back another minute. As soon as she came to a standstill, he tore

FORTESCUE AND ROSES AND BIRDSEYE

off the horse-blanket and, dropping to the ground, ran as fast as his short legs could carry him into the kitchen, and disappeared.

The Colonel, who was watching from the window, tapped his approval on the window-pane. Fortescue then mounted, and, riding off some distance in the field, came back at a swinging gallop, and Birdseye took the paling most beautifully in her stride, flying over it like a bird. Betty immediately fell deeply in love with Birdseye, and declared that she must go upstairs and put on her habit, and test the horse for herself. In a little while, she came down, more bewitching than ever to Fortescue's eyes, in her trim black habit and little beaver hat.

Fortescue, mindful of Colonel Beverley's scrutiny, put Betty on horseback in the old way, by taking her slim foot in his hand, and Betty stiffening her knee and rising into the side-saddle, which had been put on Birdseye's back. Betty did the standing leap beautifully half a dozen times, and then, riding off in the field, turned and came back, and Birdseye made a running leap like the flight of a lapwing. Fortescue had no doubt that Betty was quite safe by her own horsemanship on Birdseye's back. They were so interested in their pastime that they forgot the passing of the hours. The Christmas dinner at Holly

BETTY'S VIRGINIA CHRISTMAS

Lodge was served at four o'clock, and just before the hour Uncle Cesar came out of the house and said with a courtly bow to Fortescue:

"Ole Marse, he say it is mos' fou' o'clock, an' you mus' come in an' have Christmas dinner with Miss Betty an' him."

Fortescue demurred a little, meaning all the while to accept. His riding clothes were hardly suitable, he said. But Betty clinched the matter by saying to Uncle Cesar:

"Tell the Colonel that Mr. Fortescue will stay to dinner, and hopes his riding clothes will be excused."

There was just time for Betty to skip upstairs and jump into a little gown of a pale and jocund yellow, with an open neck, around which she hung the Colonel's Christmas gift, the little locket. The elbow sleeves showed her dimpled arms, and with deliberate coquetry she put in her shining hair one of the white roses Fortescue had brought her, and another over her innocent and affectionate little heart. When she entered the sitting-room, which served also as a dining-room, Betty was justly triumphant. She knew that she was looking her best.

CHAPTER VIII
THE SHADOW OF THE PAST

There was not much money at Holly Lodge, but Christmas dinners were ridiculously cheap, and some of earth's choicest products lay almost at the door of the little house. Fortescue thought he had never seen so noble a turkey or such captivating oysters, and when the plum pudding was brought in with a sprig of holly stuck in it and surrounded by a sea of fire, he hypocritically pretended he had never before seen anything like it.

He settled the question of his absence from Rosehill and his guests, by saying debonairly:

BETTY'S VIRGINIA CHRISTMAS

"Those fellows at Rosehill will get along all right. With a soldier, one must catch pleasure on the wing. And every one of the fellows would stay, just as I do, if they had half a chance."

"That was the way the youngsters talked in my time," said the Colonel, laughing. "War and the ladies, eh?"

The Colonel grew reminiscent of past Christmas days.

"I recollect one in particular," he said grimly: "the Christmas of '64 in the trenches at Petersburg, when it was snowing and freezing and hailing, and we had nothing to eat, and death and defeat stalked with us. Don't you remember that Christmas, boy?" asked the Colonel of Uncle Cesar.

"God knows I does," responded Uncle Cesar fervently.

"That boy," continued the Colonel, indicating the gray-haired Cesar, "was my body-servant during the whole war. He is an arrant coward, and would run away if he thought there was a Yankee within five miles."

Uncle Cesar bore this imputation upon his personal courage with a broad grin.

"I warn't no soldier-man, ole Marse," he explained. "I was jes' your body-servant, and I was skeered of Yankees, and I'se skeered of 'em now."

THE SHADOW OF THE PAST

At this, Fortescue laughed.

"You needn't be afraid of me, Uncle Cesar," he said.

But Uncle Cesar shook his head.

"Yankees is mighty cu'rrus. In the wartime, they jes' as soon kill a man as wring a chicken's neck."

"But I must say," added the Colonel, "that although Cesar always disappeared promptly as soon as we got into a dangerous place, he invariably turned up when the trouble was over, and with something hot for me to eat or something to drink—which he called coffee, and was almost as good."

"'Twuz parched corn, an' taters cut up an' roasted. An' mos' in gineral, I could find somebody's cow to milk for ole Marse," Uncle Cesar added with another grin.

The Colonel chuckled at this.

"That black rascal, sir," he said, indicating the faithful and devoted servitor, "could milk a cow into a bottle and never spill a drop. But there weren't any cows to rob in the trenches around Petersburg that Christmas day of '64, eh, boy?"

The Colonel's tone was joking, but in his eyes, as they met those of his gray-haired "boy," was a sombre expression. The bygone tragedy rose before the old soldier and his "boy." Once more they saw the pinched

BETTY'S VIRGINIA CHRISTMAS

faces of the starving soldiers, the scanty portions of miserable food, the agonies of cold and hunger, and from the far-off years came back the sullen booming of the cannon, the frightful shriek of the bursting shells, the cracking of bullets. "In the trenches"—the phrase was enough to raise gruesome ghosts and awful phantoms from their bloody graves.

It was Betty who brought the two old men away from sad Christmas memories.

"Well, Granddaddy," she said, "it's all over now, thank heaven, and we have everything to be proud of on both sides. I am so glad that I am a soldier's daughter, and so proud when I can say so."

At that, Fortescue, who quickly adopted the quaint and old-fashioned customs of people like Colonel Beverley and Betty, rose from the table and gave Betty a military salute, which delighted her beyond words.

When dinner was over, Betty insisted that Fortescue should instruct her in the manual of arms, and, with a broomstick for a gun, Betty went through with the whole manual, to the Colonel's intense delight.

"By George!" he cried. "She would make a magnificent recruit!"

It was then growing dusk, and the Colonel reminded Betty that it was the usual hour she always sang to her harp for him. Fortescue

HER GRACEFUL FIGURE MAKING TO FORTESCUE THE PRETTIEST PICTURE HE HAD EVER SEEN

THE SHADOW OF THE PAST

took the green baize cover off the harp, and Betty played and sang, her graceful figure and lovely, rounded arms making to Fortescue the prettiest picture he had ever seen.

She had a sweet, untrained voice, like a bird in the forest, and sang to perfection the old-fashioned, sentimental songs the Colonel loved.

Six o'clock came all too soon, and Fortescue, forced to remember his duties as host, at last reluctantly rose to go. They were, however, to meet in a few hours at the Red

BETTY'S VIRGINIA CHRISTMAS

Plains ball. As Fortescue galloped along the frozen road between Holly Lodge and Rosehill, he thought he had never had so pleasant a Christmas day. It was all simple and innocent pleasure, like the pastimes of children, but it was not the less joyous and satisfying on that account. Fortescue came to the conclusion that a great deal of beauty, joy, charm, goodness, and merriment, and even the sublime thing called "happiness," might be found in a little brown house with one sitting-room and one chimney, and on a place with only one cow and one horse.

CHAPTER IX

LOVE AND THE CHASE

While Betty was dressing, with Aunt Tulip as lady's maid, for the Red Plains party, the subject of Kettle was under discussion.

"That chile," said Aunt Tulip, "went an' hide hisself as soon as he got offen Mr. Fortescue's hoss, an' when I went to hunt fur him, if you believe me, Miss Betty, I foun' him way up in the lof' over the kitchen, trimblin' like a leaf, an' he wouldn't come down 'twell he see Mr. Fortescue had done rode away. Then he tell Cesar he could milk, an' he tooken the bucket an' went out an' milk ole Bossy as good as ever you see a cow milked in your life, an' he brung in enough wood fur the whole house, an' help Cesar to feed ole Whitey. That boy is mighty industr'ous.''

This was encouraging news, and induced Betty to think that Kettle would certainly be worth his keep.

At half past eight, Sally Carteret, in the big family carriage, came for Betty, and the two girls drove over to Red Plains. The ball was a replica of the dance at Marrowbone. It is not often in life that one can live over so much as a single hour of happiness, but Betty lived over a whole evening of joy. There was Fortescue, who claimed her hand ruthlessly for many dances, and his brother officers, who were scarcely less fascinating to Betty, and the University students, who assumed great intimacy upon short acquaintance, and old friends, with whom she had danced at dancing school. And there was the same merriment and the same music—Isaac Minkins and Uncle Cesar with their fiddles, and the colored youth with his "lap organ" —and the same kind of supper, the same kind of eggnog, and the same songs, and the same hearty Christmas spirit. The dance, though, did not last so late, as the hunt would begin

LOVE AND THE CHASE

early in the morning, and Betty was back at Holly Lodge and in bed by two o'clock. She had warned Aunt Tulip not to disturb herself so early to make a fire for Betty to dress by, but to send Kettle. At half past five, Kettle knocked at Betty's door, and in two minutes a gorgeous fire called Betty from her bed. At six o'clock in the wintry morning, just as Betty was pulling on her gauntlets, she heard the tramp of horses' hoofs under her window. Uncle Cesar had the side-saddle ready, and when Betty went downstairs, Fortescue was tightening the girths on Birdseye. As the Colonel was not there to watch, Fortescue, in the darkness, took Betty's slender waist in his hands and swung her, by the modern fashion, into the saddle. Although it was still cold, the icy grip had moderated a little, and the ground was clear. Betty and Fortescue galloped along in the ghostly darkness, saying little, but with a delightful feeling of nearness and aloneness.

The day was breaking when they dismounted before the great portico at Bendover. The huntsmen were gathering rapidly, and there were several ladies to join the hunt. Negro boys were leading the steaming horses up and down, while the huntsmen passed into the hospitable house. Breakfast was smoking on the table, and there was a constant

BETTY'S VIRGINIA CHRISTMAS

procession of hot coffee from the kitchen, with the inevitable five kinds of bread which Virginia hospitality imperatively requires for breakfast. There were so many dishes that the long table would not accommodate them, and there was a semicircle of oysters, sausage, deviled bones, and other substantials around the broad open hearth. The breakfast, though plentiful, was hurried, so that the start could be made before the sun dried the rime off the ground. Everybody laughed and talked and nobody listened. In half an hour they were crowding out upon the lawn to mount. As it was a Christmas hunt, every horse carried in his headstall a sprig of holly berries. Of the half-dozen girls present, each had her special cavalier, Fortescue, of course, being the escort of Betty on her new mount. The hounds, impatient to be off, yelped fretfully as they trotted about with their noses to the ground, sniffing eagerly. The horses, knowing what was up, were keen to stretch their legs. That day's quarry was to be a very astute old red fox, which had devastated many chicken-coops in the smaller homesteads in the highlands, as the slightly rolling country beyond the river shore was called.

At last the hunt was off for a screeching run. About four miles from Bendover, Rat-

LOVE AND THE CHASE

tler, the Nestor of the pack of hounds, caught the scent, and, lifting his head, gave one short, loud yelp of triumph, and then dashed away, making straight for a straggling skirt of woods. There was a rough cart-road through

it, and along this the huntsmen galloped, the dogs crying near to them. Fortescue rode close to Betty's pommel. Birdseye maintained her character, and Betty thought she had never known so good a mount. It had been Fortescue's expectation that Betty would be merely a spectator of the hunt, but with such a horse as Birdseye under her Betty rode straight and followed the hounds. The scent lay across the open fields and straggling woodlands, and was not particularly rough, but Betty took all that came in her way. Birdseye was naturally a beautiful jumper, and, like many horses, took to the

BETTY'S VIRGINIA CHRISTMAS

sport with joy. Fortescue admired Betty's lithe figure on the galloping horse, her delicate cheeks deeply flushed, and the little vagrant tendrils of hair, escaped from her filmy veil, streaming upon the air.

There was a roaring run of an hour, and then, in the midst of an open place in the woods, the scent was lost. The huntsmen pulled up, and the hounds, at fault, rushed

whimpering from one spot to another. The horses were breathed, but Birdseye's wind, like everything else about her, was admirable, and she was impatient to be off again. After half an hour of uncertainty, the hounds running hither and yon, the trail was again struck, and the whole pack, led by Rattler, went shrieking on their way, in full cry. There was another hour's hard run, and then, close to a little farmhouse, and on the

LOVE AND THE CHASE

edge of the poultry yard where the red fox had found his prey, he met the doom of justice. The dogs closed in upon him, and although the fox, vicious to the last, snarled and bit furiously, the day of vengeance was at hand. At that moment every huntsman put spurs to his horse, that he might be first in at the death, but to Fortescue this honor came. The master of the hunt rode up and dismounted. There was no ceremony of throwing his whip upon the ground, for the foxes were really pests, and were meant to be destroyed. The scoundrel fox by that time lay dead upon the ground, and the master handed his knife to Fortescue, who cut off the brush, a splendid one, thick and long. Betty's heart beat as she rode up with the others. The master was on the ground, patting and encouraging the dogs. Fortescue was also on the ground. The presentation of the brush could not take place until it had been washed and prepared, but a word or two and a look from Fortescue's laughing eyes conveyed to Betty that she was to receive the honor.

CHAPTER X

THE FLYING FEET OF THE DANCERS

It was now after ten o'clock, and, although they had ridden a good fifteen miles, much of it had been in a circle, and they were not more than five miles from Bendover. Sally Carteret led the procession back to Bendover, along the country roads, in the clear wintry noon. The farmers and their wives came running out to their gates to know if the fox was killed, and rejoiced to know that he was dead on the very scene of his iniquities.

The sharp air and the exciting exercise had fired the blood of all. They laughed and sang,

THE FEET OF THE DANCERS

and the gentlemen complimented the ladies upon their pluck, and got compliments in return. Fortescue thought that the clock of the centuries had turned back—it was so quaint, so old-fashioned. The modern, eager, bus-

tling, anxious world was forgotten; it was like the hunting and hawking of the eighteenth century.

The cavalcade rode onto the lawn at Bendover soon after twelve o'clock. Other guests had arrived by that time, and then was served the real hunt breakfast. The hunting people had the keen appetites that are bred by five hours in the saddle on a wintry day, and swarmed merrily into the dining-room, where the long table was again set out with the inevitable deviled turkey, oysters, old hams, and all the seductions of a Virginia hunt breakfast. When at last breakfast was over, the brush, which had been cleaned and rudely mounted in a wooden splint, was brought in, and Fortescue, with a little speech presented it to Betty. Then, somebody began the old hunting song of "John Peel," which accompanies the ceremony of presenting the brush, and a rousing chorus rang out—it is easy to start a rousing chorus at Christmas time in Virginia, especially when the memory of John Peel is recalled at a Christmas hunt.

"D' ye ken John Peel, d' ye ken John Peel,
    With his horse and his hounds in the morning?
His view-halloo will awaken the day,
    Or the fox from his lair in the morning."

Sally Carteret went to the piano in the drawing-room and began to play a waltz. That was enough. In half a minute every girl in the party was waltzing with her cavalier, in the big uncarpeted hall. The girls who had ridden to the hounds tucked up their short riding-skirts and danced energetically, for a Virginia girl is born and lives dancing. Of course, Fortescue had the first waltz with Betty, and saw in her eyes a shy kindness that thrilled him. When Sally Carteret had done her duty at the piano, another girl took her

THE FEET OF THE DANCERS

place conscientiously, and gave Sally her chance with the gentlemen, especially Sheldon, one of the young officers who were guests at Rosehill, and who had developed an admiration for Sally scarcely inferior to Fortescue's for Betty Beverley.

The dancing kept up for an hour or two, but as there was a ball ahead for that night, and for every night that week, the party dispersed by three o'clock. Some went home, others were quartered in the neighborhood, for the Virginia houses were always wide open to guests for the night as well as for the day.

Betty, with the fox-brush fastened to her pommel, rode back in triumph to Holly Lodge, escorted by Fortescue and his three guests. The Colonel hobbled out with his stick to greet Betty, and afar off down the little lane Betty saw him, and waved the brush at him triumphantly. When the party rode up to the little porch, Fortescue flung himself off his horse and assisted Betty.

"See, Granddaddy!" cried Betty, running up the steps and shaking the brush at the Colonel. "Mr. Fortescue won it and gave it to me."

"Most complimentary of Mr. Fortescue," said the Colonel, giving a splendid military salute to Fortescue.

BETTY'S VIRGINIA CHRISTMAS

The Colonel was glad that his little granddaughter had received the compliment, because, being more worldly wise than Betty, he understood what the fall meant from Rosehill to Holly Lodge. But the kind and hospitable county people saw no difference, and Betty

Beverley of Holly Lodge received the same attentions as Betty Beverley of Rosehill.

The Colonel invited the young officers in to have a toddy, to which they promptly agreed, eating and drinking and dancing being obligations of a high order in that community. The Colonel, standing grandly, glass in hand, gave his favorite toast:

"Gentlemen, accept the assurances of my distinguished consideration."

THE FEET OF THE DANCERS

Then, with many promises to meet again that evening, and engagements for dances, Fortescue and his friends mounted and rode away, and Betty, after telling the Colonel the incidents of the hunt, went up to her little room to catch a few hours of sleep; for sleep had to be caught at odd times during Christmas week.

Again that night and every night was a dance, each a repetition of the other, for there was not much room for variety, and the same resources were at the command of all. Fortescue, imbibing the hearty spirit of the community, longed, as he had said at Holly Lodge, to have a ball at Rosehill, but a certain delicacy and tenderness toward Betty and the Colonel hindered him. He did not like to assume too quickly the rôle of the master of Rosehill, and, then, a dream was dawning upon him of a ball at Rosehill, where

Betty should be the chatelaine and receive with him. They made great strides toward intimacy, and once in the maze of the last waltz before daybreak Fortescue chose to forget the "Miss" to Betty's name and in her ear called her "Betty." Betty pretended not to hear it, but it thrilled her from head to foot.

Fortescue was no laggard in love, but he had the chivalrous, old-fashioned notion that a girl was to be courted, and that he had to show his devotion in other ways than by many dances with Betty and visits to Holly Lodge before he could dare to ask Betty for the royal treasure of her love. Perhaps, he thought, in six months, by showing her unvarying attention and remembrance, he might dare to speak the winged word, and possibly Betty might then condescend to listen to him. For Fortescue, in a simple, manly way, was as unsophisticated as Betty. Moreover, he had a deadly fear of the Colonel, and considered that he had entered upon a regular campaign, instead of merely attempting a sortie upon the enemy.

On the afternoon before Fortescue's leave was up, he proposed a skating party upon the frozen river. There were few skaters among the girls, for the river and ice-ponds were not frozen often enough to incline them to the

THE FEET OF THE DANCERS

sport. Betty, however, could skate prettily, especially with Fortescue's arm to support her. They were in full sight of the windows of Holly Lodge, the Colonel, who knew the ice in that latitude was treacherous, keeping his eye upon the figures darting back and forth upon the river. Betty, in a little red hood, was bewitching. Sally Carteret was the only other girl skater, and they had so many cavaliers that it was difficult to have a private word with any.

Late in the afternoon, Fortescue and his friends had to take the steamboat which had so frightened Kettle, on the greater river, where the channel was kept open. The parting with Betty was supposed to occur on the river-bank, when Betty took the path to the little brown house, and Fortescue went to Rosehill to start for the landing. Fortescue had time, however, to escort Betty to the edge of the little lawn at Holly Lodge. They talked of the merry, idle, pleasant nothings which make up the staple of youth, until they reached the edge of the lawn. The Colonel, narrowly watching his one ewe lamb, saw only Fortescue's low bow, his hat in his hand, and knew nothing of the look in his eyes, and the tender pressure of Betty's hand, and his brief, significant words.

"I wouldn't go," he said, "if my leave

BETTY'S VIRGINIA CHRISTMAS

were not up; but I am a soldier, and a soldier must obey orders. Promise that you won't forget me."

It was just at the hour that one week before Betty had landed from the table in Fortescue's arms, but in that time a new heaven and a new earth had revealed themselves to both of them. Betty was a constitutional and incurable coquette, but deep in her heart she was the soul of sincerity.

"I won't forget you," she said softly, and Fortescue, turning and walking rapidly back to Rosehill, felt a profound satisfaction, a delicious confidence, that was in itself happiness. How faithful was Betty to the gallant old Colonel! This reflection brought some perplexities into Fortescue's mind, but he dismissed them, as sturdy young soldiers of twenty-five can throw out of doors unwelcome guests in the guise of unwelcome thoughts.

CHAPTER XI
THE DREAM OF LOVE

The Christmas festivities closed with a bang, the visitors departed, and the county settled down to dullness between the new year and the springtime. Those of the young people who could, went away to the cities for the gay season. Betty Beverley was left very much alone, but this she did not mind. Indeed, it was rather a respite to her. Betty, like all her kind, had a heart, and was brimming over with emotions. Until that Christmas-time, her heart and her emotions had been her sport, and she had gone upon her cruel path distributing smiles and downcast glances and pretty phrases impartially, among many admirers. But the coquette always comes to grief at last, and is throttled when the great master passion awakes. Betty was still coquettish to all the world except to Fortescue. It is true he had not asked her outright to marry him, but Betty rather liked the graduated steps toward the ultimate heights of joy. Being a confident creature, she had no doubt that Fortescue was hers, but she was quite willing to put off the time when the unseen bonds should become the visible chain. For these Southern coquettes develop naturally into devoted and adoring wives, with no eyes for any man but one.

There had been glorious winter weather up to New Year, but within a week the January storms set up, and for two months there was sleet and snow. The small brown house was

shut in, and there was little passing back and forth among the county people. The bad weather kept Betty at home many Sundays from the old Colonial church, with its ven-

THE DREAM OF LOVE

erable rector. The Colonel's rheumatism was much encouraged by the stormy season, and he too was house-bound. In this time of solitude, Betty lived in two worlds, one the narrow walls of Holly Lodge, and the other the great and splendid world of the imagination, the Arcady of youth and love. As she looked out of her dormer window toward Rosehill, a mysterious smile shone upon her speaking face as she saw herself once more the mistress of the fine old house. It is true there was an obstacle to be got over. This was Fortescue's profession, because he had told her how a soldier was sent hither and yon. Betty was the last girl in the world to ask a man to give up his profession, and, most of all, the profession of arms, but youth and inexperience can rearrange, in theory, the pawns upon the chessboard of life.

Fortescue kept up an active siege. Every week came flowers from him, or a book, or a box of bonbons, something to remind Betty of his existence. Constantly little white notes were written by Betty, thanking him, and with a word or two of deeper meaning. Betty reckoned, as a certainty, that in the spring Fortescue would return with the officers who were to make the military survey. There would be at least a dozen officers, so Fortescue had told Betty, and they were to have a camp on the Colonel's land, only five miles away, and although there would be much work, there would also be a little play.

As Betty looked out of the window on the wintry scene, she imagined it in the first bloom of the early spring, the leaden skies turned to a sapphire blue, the frozen earth all

brown and green and odoriferous, the naked branches of the trees and shrubs were transformed into their first sweet budding, and the silver river seemed dancing in the sun. Betty was a busy little soul, and had not much time for reverie, particularly as she was hard at work on her summer clothes, making dainty little muslin frocks for herself, which she could do very well. But there was a magic hour in her own little room after she was ready for bed, when the candles were out and only the scarlet and golden glory of the firelight shone upon her. Then Betty, in a smart little rose-colored dressing gown,

THE DREAM OF LOVE

which was the pride of her heart, would huddle against the dormer window that looked toward Rosehill, and think thoughts and dream dreams.

CHAPTER XII

KETTLE ACTS HIS OWN ILIAD

It was, on the whole, a happy, though solitary winter, and a very comfortable one to others at Holly Lodge, besides Betty. The comfort was to a great degree brought about by Kettle. The boy not only picked up chips and made the fires, and churned, and milked the one cow, but was helpful at every turn to Uncle Cesar and Aunt Tulip. The first thing had been to provide him with some warm clothes, and by the united efforts of Betty and Aunt Tulip this had been accomplished. Then, one bitter day, when there was nobody to go for the mail to the village post-office,

KETTLE ACTS HIS OWN ILIAD

two miles away, Kettle, without saying a word to anybody, slipped off. He knew that Betty, whom he adored, was always looking for letters, and Kettle, in his little heart, determined that she should not look in vain that day. He was missed, and Aunt Tulip resigned herself to the belief that the boy had run away again, carrying with him a much better outfit than that with which he had arrived. But Aunt Tulip's unjust suspicions were falsified when in an hour or two Kettle turned up again with the Colonel's weekly newspaper and a letter and a large box of sweets for Betty, from a source which she knew very well. Aunt Tulip gave Kettle a wigging for "runnin' off 'thout tellin' nobody," but he was merely admonished not to go again without giving notice. The expedition, however, turned out to be very profitable for Kettle, as the keeper of the country store, who was also the postmaster, had engaged Kettle in conversation, and had ended by presenting him with two shirts of a gaudy pink, and a cap, which saved Kettle's one hat for Sundays.

Aunt Tulip was a pessimist on the subject of boys, and was always expecting an outbreak of depravity on Kettle's part. The form in which this came was altogether unusual. Kettle loved music, and whatever he

BETTY'S VIRGINIA CHRISTMAS

might be doing, if he heard the strains of the Colonel's violin, or especially Betty's touch upon the harp in the sitting-room, it would have been necessary to chain him up to keep him away. He would sit on a little cricket in a corner, his black, shiny eyes full of rapture, and his mouth one vast grin. Kettle was in a heaven of delight when the Colonel, of evenings, tuned up his violin, and, sending for Uncle Cesar, "ole Marse" and his "boy" would make sweet, old-time music between them. In a little while, however, Kettle began to long that he too might call the soul of music forth from the strings. On the rare occasions when the Colonel was able to go out for a walk, or when he was taking his afternoon nap more soundly than usual, Kettle would creep to the fiddle-case, and, opening it, would let his little black hand wander among the strings, and, bending his ear down, he would listen as if it were the music of the spheres. Uncle Cesar caught him at this one day, and, seizing him by the collar, gave him a shaking which made Kettle's teeth rattle. Kettle shrieked, and Betty came running into the kitchen, expecting to find a tragedy in progress.

"Miss Betty," said Uncle Cesar, "this heah impident little black nigger has been openin'

KETTLE ACTS HIS OWN ILIAD

ole Marse' fiddle-box an' mine, and pickin' at the strings, an' I kinder believe he has been a-pickin' at the strings of your harp, Miss Betty. Did you ever heah of such owdaciousness sence Gord made you, Miss Betty?"

"No, I never did," answered Betty promptly. And then she said sternly, with an accusing forefinger, to Kettle:

"Remember, Kettle, if ever I catch you meddling with the harp or with the violin, I will certainly give you a good switching, myself. Do you understand?"

"Yessum," answered Kettle, with solemn emphasis.

This engagement was reinforced by Uncle Cesar promising him an additional switching in case he did not get his deserts in the first one.

For a week or two, Kettle was able to keep his fingers off the harp-strings and out of the fiddle-box, but one morning, when the winter sun was shining, and Colonel Beverley had gone out for a little turn on the lawn, Kettle fell from grace. Suspicious sounds were heard in the sitting-room. Aunt Tulip softly opened the door, and there was Kettle down on his knees before the fiddle-case, picking away in rapture. Aunt Tulip grabbed him, and called wrathfully to Uncle Cesar to go and get a switch. Uncle Cesar, full of vengeance, went out and returned with what might better be described as a sapling, it was so long and stout. Just then Betty entered

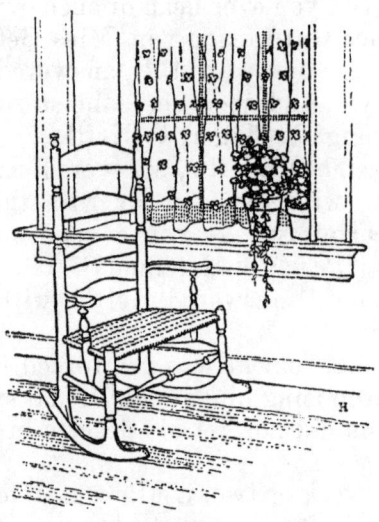

the room, and Aunt Tulip told her of Kettle's felonious acts.

"Of course, Aunt Tulip, you must give him a whipping," said Betty positively.

The whole party then marched into the kitchen, and Kettle was ordered to take off his jacket, which he did with much natural reluctance. Then, Aunt Tulip, flourishing the long switch around, proceeded to harangue Kettle indignantly:

KETTLE ACTS HIS OWN ILIAD

"Ain't you 'shamed yourself, you good-for-nothin' little nigger, after all ole Marse an' Miss Betty done for you, ter sneak in the settin'-room, an' be ruinin' ole Marse' fiddle-strings, an' meddlin' with Miss Betty's harp? I tell you what, boys has got ter git switched sometimes, an' I'm agwine ter give you a switchin' this day you will remember to the Day of Judgment."

With this awful preamble, Aunt Tulip raised the switch, and Kettle, before a single stroke had descended, burst into howls. Aunt Tulip's hand faltered.

"I declar, Miss Betty," she said apologetically, pausing with the uplifted switch in the air, "it's mighty hard ter give a switchin' ter a chile as ain't got no father nor mother; but Kettle cert'ny ought to have it, an' I think Cesar kin give it ter him better'n I kin."

With this, the switch was handed over to Uncle Cesar. Kettle redoubled his yells. The prospect of the switch in Uncle Cesar's stalwart arm was indeed terrifying. Uncle Cesar, to make the ceremony more impressive, took off his coat and rolled up his shirt-sleeves, and lifted the switch on high. But it did not come down on Kettle's back when it was expected. Uncle Cesar's hand began to tremble.

"It's mighty cur'rus, Miss Betty," said

BETTY'S VIRGINIA CHRISTMAS

Uncle Cesar, hesitating and rubbing his arm, "but I kinder got my hand out with switchin' boys, an' the rheumatiz is right bad this mornin'. Anyhow, I reckon I better put off this heah switchin' 'twell the rheumatiz gits better."

"It can't be put off, Uncle Cesar," answered Betty decisively. "The truth is, Aunt Tulip and you are squarmish about giving Kettle what he deserves. Now, I believe in discipline, and if you promise a boy a switching, you ought to give it to him. So give me the switch."

The instrument of torture was duly handed over to Betty. Kettle suddenly stopped his wailings, and his mouth came wide open as if it were on hinges. Betty, too, by way of nerving herself for the task, began to give Kettle a lecture.

"Now, Kettle," she said sternly, "your conduct has been perfectly outrageous. You were told not to touch my harp or the violins."

"I know it, Miss Betty," whimpered Kettle, his arm to his eyes, "but them fiddles, they jes' seem a-callin' an' a-callin' ter me fur ter come an' play on 'em an' that air harp—Miss Betty, ef I could play a chune on one of them fiddles, I'd ruther do it—I'd ruther do it——"

Kettle's imagery failed him in finding a simile strong enough.

KETTLE ACTS HIS OWN ILIAD

"But you were told not to touch them, and you disobeyed. Now you are going to get a whipping for it," replied Betty, catching her under lip in her little white teeth, and raising once more the five-foot and inch-thick switch. When it had been lifted above him before, Kettle had bawled loudly, but at the sight of Betty standing on tiptoe with the switch grasped in both hands, Kettle's open mouth suddenly extended in a huge grin, and he burst into a subdued guffaw. In vain, Betty held the switch aloft and tried to screw up courage to bring it down on Kettle. It was quite impossible with Kettle grinning before her and chuckling openly. Betty herself suddenly burst out laughing, and dropped the switch.

"The only thing I can think of to do with you, Kettle," she said, "is to teach you to play the fiddle."

At that, Kettle's mouth, if possible, came wider open than ever.

"Lord, Miss Betty!" he cried, "does you mean you is a-gwine to put the bow in my han' and lemme scrape them strings with it?"

"Yes, indeed," answered Betty. "I will teach you your notes, and Uncle Cesar will show you how to handle the bow."

From that day began Kettle's musical education. The Colonel sitting in his great chair, would smile at Betty with the music-book, instructing Kettle in the notes which she knew. Kettle was extremely stupid at learning his notes, and Betty frequently promised him the long delayed switching for his negligence. But as soon as Uncle Cesar took charge of him and put the bow in his hand, Kettle learned with amazing rapidity.

"I am afraid, my dear," the Colonel would say to Betty on these occasions, "that Kettle can master the concrete better than the abstract. However, he must learn his notes."

Kettle progressed so fast that in the course of a couple of months he enjoyed the privilege of playing a second to the Colonel's fiddle. The boy's arms were barely long enough to use a grown-up fiddle. As he played, he shuffled about in rapture, and Betty taught him to do the back-step and double shuffle while he played. It was a new amusement in the Colonel's quiet life to have Kettle come in the sitting-room in the evening after supper, and play and dance for him, while Kettle enjoyed the performance beyond words.

CHAPTER XIII

IT WAS THE SPRINGTIME

The winter slipped away, and in April the little camp was to be formed, and the officers were to remain for a couple of months. The thought of seeing Fortescue again, brought the eloquent blood to Betty's delicate cheeks and a new brilliance to her sparkling eyes. The spring came early in that latitude, and the first day of April was deliciously mild. Betty was at work in the little old-fashioned garden of Holly Lodge. She had brought with her from Rosehill many rosebushes and a bed of cowslips and violets. With a garden trowel in her hand, her skirts pinned up, and a red Tam o'Shanter pushed back from her forehead, Betty was busy digging about the rose-bushes. Kettle had been of the greatest service in making the garden.

BETTY'S VIRGINIA CHRISTMAS

That morning he had been sent to the post-office for the mail, and Betty was watching out for him: he was likely to bring her a letter from Fortescue. Presently, Kettle appeared crossing the little lawn, and passed through the garden gate. His shrewd little mind had discovered that when he delivered to Betty a large, square envelope, addressed in a certain masculine handwriting, Betty was sure to smile and open the letter quickly. This happened again, but Kettle was amazed to see Betty's dimple suddenly disappear, her bright eyes suddenly grow sombre, and the color drop swiftly out of her cheeks. She read the letter through slowly, and then stood with her eyes fixed upon the ground and her lips trembling. Fortescue was not coming with the other officers. He had just received orders to the other side of the continent. He had asked for twenty-four hours' leave, which would give him a chance to see Betty for about two hours the next day. He did not know, however, whether he could get permission in time to make the boat or not, but he would do it if mortal man could. He hoped Betty would understand why he came. The girl knew well enough what he meant, but the thought of three thousand miles between them for a long time, brought its pang. The fair day suddenly lost its beauty for Betty. The

IT WAS THE SPRINGTIME

vagrant breeze seemed to sigh farewell, and the sapphire sky above her would not be long the sky above Fortescue. She was roused from her painful dream by Kettle's voice,

and realized that the boy had stood motionless next her for a long time.

"Miss Betty," he asked, "what's the matter with you?"

"A great deal is the matter with me," sighed Betty, putting the letter in her pocket,

BETTY'S VIRGINIA CHRISTMAS

and resuming her digging and trimming. What did it matter whether the roses bloomed that June or not? And the violets and the cowslips could not console her for Fortescue.

Betty remained a long time in the garden that morning. Kettle followed her about like a dog, every now and then asking anxiously:
"Miss Betty, don't you feel no better?"

In spite of her sadness and disappointment, Betty was roused out of herself by Kettle's sympathy.

"I don't feel any better now, Kettle," she said. "Perhaps I shall to-morrow."

But although Betty might show her chagrin and despondency before Kettle and the rose-bushes and the violets and the cowslips, she had no intention whatever of letting anybody else see it. When she looked up and saw the Colonel coming out to take the air, pacing up and down the garden walk in the sunny spring day, Betty, who was a clever actress, put on her most smiling aspect. As the Colonel limped up and down for half an hour, his arm on Betty's shoulder, he thought he had never known her more cheerful. She told him quite naturally that she had had a letter from Mr. Fortescue, and that he was ordered to the Northwest, but, if possible, he would be at Rosehill the next day for a short time, and would come over to see them. The Colonel's

IT WAS THE SPRINGTIME

emotions concerning Fortescue were very badly mixed and perplexing even to himself. He was not so selfish as to forget Betty's happiness, and Fortescue was a fine, upstanding young fellow, quite after the Colonel's heart. But there was something calculated to daunt the brave soul of the old man in the thought of his few remaining years without Betty. He had been called upon to resign the love of his

youth, his only son, and Rosehill, and now this little one—— At the thought, the Colonel said to himself, as he had done many times in years past, amid the hail of bullets, with cannon thundering in his ears, or in snow and sleet and starvation, "Courage! Courage!"

BETTY'S VIRGINIA CHRISTMAS

All that day, Betty was in a dream. She knew very well the answer she would give Fortescue, but suddenly she looked into the stern face of Life, and saw what those dreams meant. How could she leave Holly Lodge and the Colonel and Aunt Tulip and Uncle Cesar and Kettle, and the young chickens, just hatched? Life was a practical affair with Betty, but, alas, sentiment and emotion were strong within her. She did not know how the next twenty-four hours passed, except that her eyes continually swept the narrow lane that led to the little gate of Holly Lodge. She would rather see Fortescue in the garden, and therefore dressed herself in her little pale yellow gown, and put on a great straw hat, trimmed with little yellow buds and green leaves, that was worthy of a dryad. The air was warm and soft at midday, and Betty was walking up and down the garden path, watching, watching, watching, and at last, just as she had turned her back to the gate and was walking the length of the little garden path, Fortescue was at her side. He looked so bronzed, so soldierly, so much the man, that Betty gave a little gasp of delight. There was a tall box-hedge in the little old garden which screened the walk from the windows of the house, so that Fortescue could take Betty's hand and be unseen as they walked

"BUT IF YOU LOVE ME——"

IT WAS THE SPRINGTIME

up and down in the pleasant spring noon. Then Fortescue told her all: that he had received his unexpected orders and must go, that it wrung his heart to leave her, but that he was hers forever, and that though his body might be in the far Northwest, his heart and soul would be at Holly Lodge. Betty's eyes made answer to Fortescue, and her lips spoke the winged words that gave her to her lover. A pair of robins beginning housekeeping in the grape arbor at the end of the walk sang and trilled rapturously as they watched the lovers.

There could be no question of their being married immediately, as Fortescue would be on the wing for the next four months, and he knew nothing of his new station or duties, except that both were trying and the conditions unsuited to a woman. But later, after he had seen what the conditions were, perhaps he could take Betty with him.

"I am asking a great deal of you, Betty," he said. "The wife of a junior officer has to go from place to place, to be uprooted constantly. It is true that I am lucky in having money enough to make it as easy as it can be made, still, it is hard, hard, all the same. But if you love me——"

Betty said one little word which settled that point, though her eyes were grave.

BETTY'S VIRGINIA CHRISTMAS

"How can I leave my grandfather?" she asked suddenly.

"You need not leave him," promptly replied Fortescue. "We can carry the old gentleman and the whole outfit around with us."

But Betty shook her head.

"You don't know my grandfather," she said. "He has a very independent spirit. How could a man who has lived his life here for so many years go from place to place? He must live and die here."

"He can go and live at Rosehill if he wants to," answered Fortescue, who was disposed to brush away all obstacles. "My father is pretty good to me, and he will do anything I ask him about the place."

"But Granddaddy would never consent to be a pensioner on anybody, I am sure," continued Betty, with a doleful little smile. "So

IT WAS THE SPRINGTIME

we can't be married until you are retired, thirty-six years from now."

Fortescue scouted this proposition, but he saw in Betty Beverley something that gave him pain and yet made him proud. This was a fixed loyalty to her duty. It was that which made Fortescue, who could have led a life of idle luxury, lead the stern life of a soldier. He would not have loved Betty half so well if she had shown too much willingness to cast off the old ties for the new. But, as Fortescue told himself and Betty, there are a great many troublesome questions coming up all the time concerning human beings, horses, cows, gardens, and everything else. There was one small scrap of comfort. It was,

"And the only thing is, Betty," he said, "that we shall love each other and stand by each other, and some way out of it will be found."

It was possible that in December, when the great Northwest was snow-bound, Fortescue might get a month's leave. If he came to Virginia and back, it would give him a week, perhaps ten days, at Rosehill. Of course, he would have to spend a day or two with his father and brothers but they could meet him somewhere on the way.

"I've got a fine old dad," Fortescue said, "and he is always saying that the men of to-day have no devotion to women; so the old gentleman wouldn't think me game if I didn't spend most of my leave with you, eh, Betty?"

It seemed to them but a little space of time that they had been in the garden together, when Fortescue, suddenly looking at his watch, found that he had barely time to go into the house and speak to the Colonel and then catch the boat at the landing. The friendly hedge that had screened the lovers witnessed the last throbbing kiss. Outwardly serene, but inwardly palpitating, they went quickly into the house. Betty had warned Fortescue, as they ran down the garden path, to say nothing to her grandfather.

"It will only distress him and keep him awake at night, and I will choose a time to tell him."

"All right," answered Fortescue. "Just give me notice, and I will write him the conventional letter. But to tell you the truth, Betty, I would just as soon be out of the way when the Colonel turns those pathetic eyes on you, as you talk about getting married."

Colonel Beverley had seen so many young men walking up and down the garden path with Betty, and had watched the rise and fall of so many flirtations, that he attached little consequence to Fortescue's visit. He was sorry that the young officer would not be

IT WAS THE SPRINGTIME

among the party in the camp, and added with a grim smile that no doubt the young ladies in the county would miss him extremely and would be forced to take comfort in other second lieutenants, just as it had been in his day. Then with best wishes and a handshake, and a soft pressure of Betty's fingers, Fortescue was gone.

"A fine, personable youngster," said the Colonel to Betty. "Very creditable of him, serving in the army, and he the son of a rich man. He could be, if he wished, of the idle rich."

"If he were an idle rich man, I don't think I should care much about him," said Betty significantly.

CHAPTER XIV
PROBLEMS

Up to that point, life had been the simplest of propositions to Betty Beverley, but from that day it became painfully complex. She had thought but little and spoken less of the great word "duty," but she had in her the soul of the soldier, and her duty loomed large before her, as it did before Fortescue. On this point their understanding was perfect. Betty, if Fortescue had been ordered into action, would have buckled his sword about his waist and bade him, with a smile, to go. In the same way, when Betty spoke of her duty to stay, Fortescue said no word to make her a traitor. But they were both young and full of hope and love, and had transcendent confidence in the future. Everything would come right, was the easy conviction of both.

PROBLEMS

Betty waited a few days to see if Fortescue's visit had roused any latent suspicions in the Colonel's mind, but, seeing it had not, one day when it was soft and mild as on the day of days when Fortescue had told her of his love, she walked in the little garden with the Colonel and told him all.

"But I don't mean to desert you, granddaddy," she said firmly. "I don't know how it is coming out, and neither does Jack"—for by that time Fortescue had become "Jack" to Betty—"but I hate a deserter, you know."

"It wouldn't be desertion, my dear," said the Colonel. "And it would be a base thing of me to spoil your life, my little Betty. But, as you say, a way will be found. Don't let us trouble about it until Christmas, then, as you say, Fortescue will try to get a leave that will give him a week at Rosehill, and we shall see. I think perhaps I could get on pretty well at Holly Lodge with Cesar and Tulip and Kettle."

"Do you mean," cried Betty indignantly, "that you could get on pretty well without me? Oh, what a wicked old grandfather you are!"

"But if you will come to see me sometimes," said the Colonel, anxious to find a way.

BETTY'S VIRGINIA CHRISTMAS

In due time the letter to the Colonel came from Fortescue, and the Colonel answered it in his dignified, old-fashioned manner. He did not wish and would not permit himself to be a bar to his granddaughter's happiness. After a time, when their affection had been tested, he would give his consent to the marriage.

The officers came, and the camp was pitched, and much work was done. Likewise, much eating, drinking, dancing, riding, boating, and picnicing with the county people. It was the old story of Christmas week transferred to spring. Betty appeared to be as keen over the lieutenants as Sally Carteret or any girl in the county, nor did she feel any qualms of conscience when two second lieutenants each told her at different times that he could not live without her. Betty was a little unfeeling toward her admirers, and her tears were but crocodile tears when she told the lieutenants that she could not leave her grandfather—except for that—— Here Betty broke down prettily, and the lieutenants were in despair. But they speedily recovered from their disappointment and found other outlets for their affections. Betty, the trifler, was serious enough, however, where Fortescue was concerned.

The spring melted into summer and on a

PROBLEMS

day black for Sally Carteret and the other gay young things in the county the camp was broken and the officers departed. Luckily, though, it was at the season when the Univer-

sity students returned to the county, bringing many of their fellow students with them, so that there was balm in Gilead. As for Betty, she was quite willing to play with the University students, as she had with the second lieutenants. But deep down in her heart they mattered little. There was only one man for her, and that was Lieutenant John Hope Fortescue.

The earth seemed brightening for all at Holly Lodge. The Colonel had learned more and more to accommodate himself to the little house and the simple surroundings, and, free from debts and duns, had great peace. Betty, whose heart had flown about like the larks and thrushes from bough to bough, had at last made its nest, and she too had great peace. Kettle turned out to be not only a solid addition to their comfort, but almost to their happiness. His sturdy little bow-legs waddled about, bringing wood and water, and doing errands. He was always cheery and helpful, but with the faults which are necessary to the typical boy. He would occasionally neglect his work for the sake of his adored fiddle, and when sent down to the river shore to catch crabs for dinner would become so absorbed in the sport that he would forget that it was merely a means to an end. One day, however, he incurred the wrath of the whole establishment at Holly Lodge. Among Betty's treasures was a great tall glass bottle of attar of roses, of which a single drop perfumed a room. Kettle, passing Betty's open door, the room being empty, saw on the dressing table the beautiful bottle in which was stored

PROBLEMS

the perfume he loved. The devil tempted him, and Kettle yielded. He slipped into the room, and, opening the bottle, rubbed its contents, a gill or two of attar of rose, into his wool.

Downstairs, a pungent odor, so strong that it was almost asphyxiating, penetrated, and as Kettle's steps were heard approaching the perfume became overpowering. The Colonel began to sneeze, and even Aunt Tulip and Uncle Cesar in the kitchen had to run out into the open air. Betty, with her handkerchief to her face, rushed into the little hall, where Kettle stood, his eyes bulging out of his head, as he too gasped and sneezed.

"You've upset my attar of rose upon your head!" screamed Betty. "Go out of doors this minute, and I'll hand you over to Uncle Cesar for a real switching this time."

By that time Aunt Tulip had dashed in from the kitchen, and, seizing Kettle by his woolly head, dragged him out of doors to the pump, calling meanwhile for Uncle Cesar, working in the garden.

"Cesar! You Cesar! Come heah right away, an' bring my big scissors. This heah wuffless little black nigger done tooken all Miss Betty's attar of rose an' done rub it into he haid, an' arter you git the scissors, cut a switch an' give him a good tunin' up."

BETTY'S VIRGINIA CHRISTMAS

This terrifying prospect entirely upset Kettle's moral balance, and he began to protest, spluttering and stuttering, as Aunt Tulip pumped water vigorously on his offending head.

"I 'clar ter goodness, I ain' never see Miss Betty's attar of rose. I ain' never tetch it."

At that, Aunt Tulip stopped pumping on Kettle long enough to shake him violently.

"Does you know where liars go?" cried Aunt Tulip indignantly. "Doan' you know nothin' 'bout the lake burnin' wid fire an' brimstone, an' the devil stan'in' by wid a red hot pitchfork, stickin' it into dem sinners?"

This awful future, the arrival of Uncle Cesar with the scissors, Aunt Tulip's merciless use of them on his wool, and Uncle Cesar's going off after a switch, brought shrieks from Kettle, as if he were being murdered by inches. Betty, in the house, hearing Kettle's screams, ran out, and Uncle Cesar reappeared at the same moment with a switch of horrifying proportions. Poor Kettle, with every scrap of wool cut off his head, leaving his skull as bare as an egg, was so drenched and frightened and woebegone, that Betty's heart melted.

"I think, Uncle Cesar," she said, "we won't give Kettle that switching to-day, though he certainly deserves it."

PROBLEMS

Uncle Cesar was loth to lay aside the instrument of torture.

"Miss Betty, you better lemme give him a dozen licks anyhow," urged Uncle Cesar. "You kyarn' raise boys 'thout licks."

But Betty demurred. Kettle, meanwhile, poured out a flood of penitential tears, and, moved by Betty's clemency, confessed that he had emptied the bottle of attar of rose on his head and rubbed it in. He even offered to produce the empty bottle to corroborate his word, which nobody doubted. However, the oft-deferred switching was once more postponed, and the improved prospects raised Kettle's spirits immediately. Half an hour afterward, when he was in dry clothes, he was as cheerful as ever, although minus his wool, and, having been sent to the wood-pile by the still indignant Aunt Tulip, was seen standing on his head in the intervals of picking up chips.

CHAPTER XV
THE BROKEN DREAM

As the sunny autumn succeeded the enchanted summer, it seemed to Betty as if a new and lovely light were over the world. Fortescue's letters, his constant gifts, the books which came often, and the music he sent her, and which Betty played and sang to her harp, were so many messages of love. Fortescue wrote that he had applied for leave, and that by making close connections he would be able to spend ten whole days at Rosehill. He meant to give a ball on Christmas Eve at Rosehill, and, as he wrote Betty, she could practise her future rôle as mistress of Rosehill. Fortescue could not manage the ball as well as the county people managed their Christmas balls. All he could do was to order the music and the supper and everything from

THE BROKEN DREAM

Baltimore, but when Betty presided at Rosehill things could be done better and in true Virginia style. He hoped to arrive some days before Christmas.

Then Betty began the pleasant process of counting the days. This she confided to the Colonel, for Betty understood, as few young things do, the yearning of the old for the confidence of the young, the delicacy felt by an old man lest he intrude upon the secrets of the young.

The two, Betty and the Colonel, tried very hard to dovetail the wishes and duties and interests of the triangle. Fortescue was the third angle.

"Any way," Betty cried, when they had reasoned out that she could not desert the Colonel, nor could she refuse to marry her lover, nor could Fortescue abandon his profession, nor could Betty abandon the idea of presiding at Rosehill—"Any way, Granddaddy, it will only be thirty-five years now before Jack is retired, and then we can all three settle down at Rosehill."

The preparations for Christmas gaieties began early, and the same round of dances and hunts and dinners and teas and festivities of all sorts was arranged.

It was the third day before Christmas, and Betty, with her skirts pinned up, her sleeves

BETTY'S VIRGINIA CHRISTMAS

turned back to her elbows, and a red silk handkerchief of the Colonel's tied around her head, was preparing the icing for the Christmas cake, when she saw Fortescue passing the window. There was no time to escape. The next minute he was in the little sitting-room, and Betty was clasped to his heart. After the first rapture of meeting, Betty made numerous apologies, unpinned her skirts, pulled down her sleeves, and removed the handkerchief from her shining hair, but Fortescue told her she did not look half so pretty as before. It was a happy hour, one of those little glimpses of the Elysian fields of the soul which come only to the young and the pure. Luckily, the Colonel was taking his afternoon stroll supported by his stick, and with Kettle as aide-de-camp in attendance. The lovers had a full hour to themselves in the violet dusk, the room only lighted by the wood fire and the pale glow of the wintry sunset. Presently, the Colonel came in and shook hands cordially with Fortescue. It was the hour when Betty sang to her harp the old songs the Colonel loved. Fortescue thought he had never seen so sweet a picture as Betty playing and singing to the harp, while the Colonel, leaning forward on his stick, listened with his soul in his eyes. Kettle, squatting tailor-fashion on the hearth, fixed his round eyes on

THE BROKEN DREAM

Betty, and his little woolly black head was motionless while she was singing.

Of course Fortescue stayed to supper, and Uncle Cesar was reinforced by Kettle, who was chief batter-cake server, and brought from the kitchen the numerous relays of hot batter-cakes, hot waffles, and hot biscuits of which the well known Virginia formula is, "Take two and butter them while they are hot." Afterward, when Kettle had had his supper, he was sent for to exhibit his accomplishments with the fiddle. Kettle played dances and sang simultaneously, his merry music delighting Fortescue, whose musical education was not above rag-time. Fortescue told about the arrangements he had made for the Christmas Eve ball at Rosehill, and Betty thought them ineffably grand.

When Kettle had been sent away, there was much talk about armies and soldiers between Fortescue and the Colonel, whose heart was ever with the fighting men. Betty listened with delight to this modern Froissart's Chronicle, and said presently:

"How glad I am to be a soldier's daughter!"

"And that's why you will make a glorious wife for a soldier," replied Fortescue impudently, at which Betty blushed all over her face and neck.

BETTY'S VIRGINIA CHRISTMAS

When Fortescue was walking back to Rosehill, he saw over his shoulder the lights shining from Betty's dormer windows. He went direct to his own room as soon as he reached Rosehill, and after a while saw the lights go out in Betty's windows. Fortescue, who, like

most soldiers, believed in God and respected Him as the Great Commander, knew that Betty was saying her simple, earnest prayers for him, and the thought that the prayers of the innocent were heard gave him a reverent thankfulness. To Betty, in her little white bed in the darkened room, with the curtain drawn wide so that she could watch the lights at Rosehill as long as they burned, it was as if the world were growing too beautiful.

THE BROKEN DREAM

Deep in her heart was the old Greek superstition that one cannot walk the airy heights of happiness long without a precipice opening beneath one's feet. The thought oppressed her and kept her awake long after the windows of Rosehill were dark. Something like a presentiment stole into her heart.

"Whatever happens, though," she thought, "nothing can come between Jack and me. We understand each other too well."

Suddenly the melancholy cry of a nightbird resounded outside in the darkness. It was strange to hear that cry at midnight in the dead of winter and it made Betty shiver.

The next day the gaieties began with great vigor. The county was full of visitors, and the whirl of dancing feet was everywhere.

Early the next day, Fortescue came over to Holly Lodge. He sat awhile in the sitting-room, talking pleasantly to the Colonel, who, in the old days before the continent was linked by railways, had travelled through the far-off country beyond the Rocky Mountains. Betty was congratulating herself upon the extreme good fortune that Fortescue and her grandfather had so much in common. But even that brought a little chill to her heart, for blessings have their price, and Betty was superstitious.

The morning was cold and clear, and after

BETTY'S VIRGINIA CHRISTMAS

awhile Fortescue asked Betty to come out for a turn with him. Betty went willingly enough. The Colonel watched the two as they started off up the lane toward the belt of woodland that skirted the highway. Betty's trim figure in black, with a little black hat on her shapely head, just came up to Fortescue's shoulder. They were a good height, and walked well together, thought the Colonel, used to watching marchers.

Of course Betty and Fortescue had everything to tell each other, in spite of the long letters which had been exchanged weekly. But when they were once in the woodland, with the morning sun shining upon the tall and scattered cedars, Fortescue threw everything aside for the chief purpose he had in view.

"Now, Betty," he said, "I have come here to have you fix the day when we shall be married. I don't believe in long engagements, and never meant to have one. My special duty will end in the spring, and then we must be married."

Betty's eyes grew troubled. What should she say? How could she leave the Colonel? Something like this she stammered out. Fortescue met it impatiently. He believed in her doing her duty by the Colonel, but, man-like, he thought that Betty must do her duty by

THE BROKEN DREAM

him first. There was no question of money. Fortescue had enough to do as he pleased.

"Make the Colonel comfortable any way you like," he said. "Let him stay at Holly Lodge or go to Rosehill. My father has given me the place, and some day, when I am a re-

tired major-general, Betty, we shall live there, you and I and our children. But we must come to a positive arrangement now."

Fortescue's tone displeased Betty. He was too confident, too much in the way of giving orders, a thing which Betty herself was accustomed to doing. It cannot be denied that Betty was a little spoiled and rather haughty. Her reply to Fortescue displeased him even more than his words had displeased her.

BETTY'S VIRGINIA CHRISTMAS

"I think," she said coldly, "that you are taking too much for granted. Some one must be considered as well as yourself."

This was a most unlucky speech. Fortescue's reply was a retaliation. They were only twenty-one and twenty-six, and although they had far more of feeling, strength, depth, and steadiness of character than young persons usually have, they were no wiser or more experienced than most young things. Some words followed, impetuous and domineering on Fortescue's part, exasperatingly cool on Betty's. They were both keen of wit, and readily surmised the meaning of sharp phrases. Fortescue's feelings were quick, and Betty had a tidy little temper of her own. Suddenly, they knew not how or when or why, but they were walking back toward Holly Lodge in the crisp winter morning, each with a resentful heart. Their first meeting as confessed sweethearts had developed into a serious quarrel. It was not about those trifling things that arise between young lovers, and which bring tears and reproaches, and then end in forgiveness, but it concerned a grave matter, the regulation of their future lives and their mutual obligations, one to the other. The question of what was to become of the Colonel had seemed so easy to settle when they had considered it on the far-off

THE BROKEN DREAM

horizon. Now, when it came close to them, it assumed a dangerous aspect. The rash and inexperienced Betty thought that it must be settled according to her ideas, and that Fortescue must wait until the Colonel was coaxed into saying what he would do in the premises. Fortescue, with a much better idea of the vicissitudes of an officer's life, saw that Betty's plans and compromises and dovetailings of duty were impracticable, and told her so. The bitterest quarrels on earth are those between a man and a woman who love each other, and whose anger "doth work like madness in the brain." It was the more intense because each felt to be in the right, and that the other must yield in the name of love and duty. But yielding was new and strange to each. Betty knew so little of the power of money that she resented Fortescue's bringing that into the discussion, and, moreover, she was an arrogant little creature and a trifle too ready for a fight. Fortescue, who had seen the great outside world unknown to Betty, knew the Spanish proverb, "God is the general, but money is His lieutenant." It took all of Betty's self-command to hold back the tears and to keep her lips from trembling. If those tears had dropped upon her cheeks and her lovely mouth had quivered, all would have been well, but Fortescue, watching her

BETTY'S VIRGINIA CHRISTMAS

sidewise, saw only her head in the air, her delicate face as firm as marble, and said to himself savagely:

"If she doesn't care, why should I?"

All at once, a horrid doubt of Betty took possession of his mind. Once, he had laughed at her outrageous flattery of other men, her open cajolery, her pretty coquetries. Suppose, after all, she had no feeling, and was making sport of his honest heart? Perhaps she had never meant to marry him, and was only amusing herself. There might be another man—at this, Fortescue ground his teeth.

They walked the whole length of the lane without speaking. When they got to the paling surrounding the little lawn of Holly Lodge, Betty spoke, but her evil genius waited upon her tongue that day.

"Of course," she said, "as we can't agree, everything is over. But if we appear unfriendly, everybody will notice it, and I do so hate to have people gabbling about me!"

"So do I," promptly assented Fortescue.

"Then," said Betty, "we must be as friendly as ever while you are in the county. Luckily, nobody knows anything, except Grandfather, and he will, of course, keep quiet. People here don't think as much of a man's attentions to a girl as you do, and

THE BROKEN DREAM

other men have danced with me quite as much as you have."

"No doubt," replied Fortescue sharply. "I think you were simply amusing yourself all the time. Well, then, I can play that game all right. Good morning."

He was off, and Betty was walking soberly into the house. The fair day had grown dark, and her heart in her breast was like a stone. Woman-like, she began to defend herself against herself:

"If he is so dictatorial as all that, we never could have got on, so perhaps it is the best thing that we found it out immediately. If a woman gives in at once to a man and never remembers what is due anybody else, she might as well be a slave!"

CHAPTER XVI

PRIDE PAYS THE PRICE

The Colonel was playing on his violin as Betty entered the sitting-room, and what he had chosen was the sad old air of "Love Not, Love Not, Ye Hapless Sons of Men." He laid down his violin, and noticed that Betty's face was pale, in spite of the sharp winter air, and that she spoke with suppressed fury in her voice.

"Grandfather," she said, "it is all over between Mr. Fortescue and me. Please don't ask me about it. We didn't disagree about a trifle, but about something important. We are perfectly friendly, and mean to keep so,

PRIDE PAYS THE PRICE

because we don't want the people in the county talking about us and worrying us with questions. But it is all over, quite over."

The Colonel started and studied Betty closely. He knew the resolute character, the stubborn pride, that lay beneath all of Betty's frivolities. She could do things as foolish as any girl of her age, but she could suffer more than most. The Colonel sighed as he looked at her pale, unsmiling face, her eyes full of angry light. He understood the sharp pain of those who have not learned the awful lesson of life, the haughty attitude of the young who have never known defeat, the sufferings of mortified pride and wounded vanity, and, above all, he had an inward conviction that Betty in her heart loved Fortescue. Man-like, the Colonel was not so sure of Fortescue, and a resentment, grim and stern, rose within him. Until the young officer appeared, Betty had been quite happy and satisfied at Holly Lodge. In time, she would have married some one in the county perhaps, and would have led that peaceful life on the sunny side of the wall, which only the quiet lives know. But with Fortescue's appearance had come the disturbing vision of a possible return to Rosehill, of a life in the great outside world, going from place to place, of the breaking of all the old ties.

Betty had asked him not to question her, but the Colonel felt justified in asking precisely one question.

"Elizabeth, has Mr. Fortescue acted dishonorably?" he inquired, straightening up his old figure, still soldierly.

"No," replied Betty promptly. "Mr. Fortescue couldn't do anything dishonorable."

"I am glad to hear it," answered the Colonel grimly. "If he had, I should have felt called upon to chastise him according to the code in which I was reared and have lived and shall die."

Betty's heart was quivering, her pride was up in arms, the whole world seemed full of tears; but when the Colonel talked about chastising Fortescue's young strength, her sense of humor overwhelmed her pain, and she suddenly laughed a little. She did not tell the Colonel the cause of her ripple of laughter, and in another minute her eyes grew sombre and her heart once more hardened against Fortescue.

"You may be quite satisfied, Grandfather," she said. "All that has happened was my own act."

Betty turned and went out of the room. Being Christmas-time, and there being no household tasks awaiting her, no sewing to

PRIDE PAYS THE PRICE

do, because she had planned that this Christmas-time should be one of perfect leisure, that she might be free to entertain her great guest, First Love, there was nothing for her to do. She went aimlessly up to her room.

Then, suddenly, she felt a sharp headache. Her mental suffering produced a physical pain. She was rather glad of it, as it gave her an excuse for keeping to her room and lying down. The little room was flooded with winter sunshine, and a pretty fire was smouldering on the hearth. Betty drew the curtains, glancing meanwhile toward Rosehill. Her

BETTY'S VIRGINIA CHRISTMAS

keen eyes caught sight of Fortescue crossing the lawn rapidly. A great buzzard was wheeling majestically over the Rosehill house, and a group of the servants, one of the men with a gun, was standing on the edge of the lawn, prepared to fire at the bird. Fortescue walked up and, taking the gun, sighted and fired, and the buzzard fell upon the roof of the house. This little act wrung Betty's heart.

"How little he cares!" she thought bitterly. "Any trifle can distract him. Well, it was better to find it out in time."

Then, for the first time, Betty turned her eyes away as the Colonel turned his away from Rosehill. She loved the place, and deep in her heart had grown the wish to preside there once more, as Fortescue's wife. It was impossible, quite impossible, now. She could not forget Fortescue—Betty was honest enough with herself to know that, and honorable enough to respect her own affection. Love is not killed in an hour or even a day. The great stretch of life ahead of her loomed before Betty's eyes as one stands on the edge of a parched desert and thinks of the weary journey across it. For Betty Beverley, the coquette, was the soul of constancy. These thoughts and many others and a racking headache drove Betty to her bed. She threw herself on it, with all the sunshine shut out of her room, just as it had been shut suddenly out of her life.

At the midday dinner, Kettle, who had almost supplanted Uncle Cesar as butler, came up, and, opening Betty's door and putting in his little woolly head, said softly:

"Miss Betty, dinner done ready."

"I can't come down to dinner," answered Betty. "Tell the Colonel that I have a bad headache. It will be better to-night, and I am going to the party just the same. But when dinner is over, Kettle, you may bring me up some tea and toast."

Kettle had never known Betty to have an ache or a pain since he had been established at Holly Lodge, and the sight of her pale face, and the weariness in her voice, frightened him. He began to argue with Betty:

"Miss Betty, you better come down ter dinner. Aunt Tulip, she done cook some of the bes' sweet 'taters you ever see in your life, Miss Betty—got sugar on 'em, an' butter too."

"I don't care for any, thank you," said Betty, her heart far away from sweet potatoes with sugar and butter.

Kettle paused for a minute in order to think of some other inducement.

"Aunt Tulip, she got a rice pudden' wid

gre't big raisins in it, mos' as big as my fist,'' urged Kettle.

"No, thank you," replied Betty absently.

But Kettle's sympathy could not be bottled up.

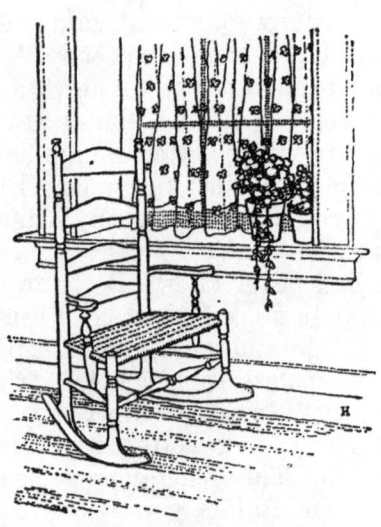

"Miss Betty," pleaded Kettle, "lemme go out an' crack you up some wun'nuts," by which Kettle meant walnuts.

Betty's patience was giving out.

"No, Kettle," she said sharply. "I don't want anything except tea and toast, as I told you."

PRIDE PAYS THE PRICE

"But, Miss Betty," persisted Kettle, edging toward the door, "I got a big bag o' chestnuts, an' they mighty good roasted on the kitchen shovel."

Betty's nerves and her temper could stand no more.

"Go away, Kettle," she cried impatiently. "Go downstairs this minute and serve the Colonel's soup."

The tone could not be mistaken, and Kettle went out of the door as if shot out of a gun. Once outside, however, his little faithful heart was still torn for Betty, and he was prepared to take great risks. He turned the door-knob noiselessly, and, putting his round, black head in the door, whispered:

"Miss Betty, Miss Betty, when I bring up yo' tea, lemme bring you up a hard b'iled aig!"

Betty's answer was to throw a pillow at Kettle, who dodged it and went clattering downstairs.

What a strange, unnatural day it was for Betty! Here in the brilliant afternoon, when she was wont to be her brightest and best, she lay huddled up in her bed, racked with physical and mental pain. Her sunny room was dark, and her active little feet felt like lead. The prospect of a party, the music, the dancing, the bright interchange of looks and words

BETTY'S VIRGINIA CHRISTMAS

that was the wine of life to Betty's pleasure-loving temperament, seemed to her now a dreadful ordeal, to be gone through with courage, and by a stupendous effort to let no one suspect the agony of her mind. Never before had she felt humiliated in the presence of any man, but she felt a sharp humiliation at the thought that in the first encounter of her will with Fortescue's, she had been defeated; whether by her own unreason or his, was equally painful. But there was no backdown in Betty, and she never dreamed of staying away from the party or giving up the fight because of an aching heart.

The old Colonel downstairs in the sitting-room felt his heart wrung for his little Betty. Too soon had come to her those shocks and disappointments against which youth rebels. The young demand happiness of life, and are in despair when they first find they cannot secure it.

Kettle, after having taken up Betty's tea, came downstairs again, and, instead of going into the kitchen, where he belonged, came into the sitting-room and, perching his small, black, and miserable self upon a little cricket, fixed his eyes upon the Colonel's grave, gray face, outlined against the window-pane. The boy sat so still and silent that the Colonel at last roused himself and asked kindly:

PRIDE PAYS THE PRICE

"What's the matter, Kettle?"

"Ain' nothin' 't all matter wid me, suh, but sumpin' is the matter wid Miss Betty, an' it kinder makes me feel bad."

The Colonel sighed; it made him feel bad, too.

All the afternoon, Kettle sat there until it was time to milk old Bossy, a duty which he had monopolized for some time past. Then there was wood and water to be brought, and all the other duties which Aunt Tulip had devised for him. But when they were over Kettle crept softly upstairs and seated himself on the top step close to Betty's door. At seven o'clock, Betty opened the door that she might call down to Aunt Tulip to assist her in getting into her gown. She almost fell over Kettle.

"What are you doing here, Kettle?"

"Jes' waitin' ter see ef you don' want nothin'," was Kettle's excuse.

The boy's inarticulate sympathy touched Betty's heart in the midst of her own unhappiness.

"I do want something," she said kindly. "I want you to tell Aunt Tulip to come here, and to bring up some more wood, and to do all sorts of things that nobody can do for me except you, Kettle."

Kettle's black face beamed. He ran downstairs after Aunt Tulip, and then began bringing wood, toiling up the stairs with as much as he could carry.

Although Betty was dressed as gaily as usual for a party, and took as much pains with her beautiful brown hair and the wreath of ivy-leaves upon it, Kettle's sharp eyes were not deceived. Something was wrong with Miss Betty.

When old Whitey pulled the rockaway up to the door, Betty came down to show herself as usual to the Colonel. The unspoken pity in his eyes moved Betty.

"Don't be afraid, Grandfather," she said. "I haven't any more cowardice in me than there is in you. I intend to be just as happy to-night as ever I was, and to dance and laugh and sing as I always do."

And then poor Betty laughed a laugh so forced, so full of pain, so unlike her usual rippling laughter, that the Colonel's heart was wrung more than ever. But he knew better than to offer Betty pity.

"Stiffen up, my dear," he said. "Life is full of disappointments. Fortescue is not the man you took him for, that is all. Put him out of your mind."

"I will," replied Betty stoutly, without the slightest ability to keep her word in the matter.

PRIDE PAYS THE PRICE

Driving along the hard country road in the wintry night, Betty thought of all those things she might do by which a headstrong, proud, and deeply sensitive girl may inflict pain upon herself as well as another. She would, of course, give Fortescue back his ring that night, and the next day there were to be re-

turned a few trifles other than books and flowers that he had sent her. The ring was a simple thing, a little ruby heart surrounded with small pearls. She had never worn it in public, for fear it might attract attention—people in the country are observant of trifles. But she loved the little ring as a symbol.

That night the party was at Red Plains, and Betty knew she would meet the whole county. There was no hall for dancing at Red Plains, but the drawing-room was cleared of furniture, and there the dancing went on. As Betty entered the drawing-room, almost the first person she saw was Fortescue danc-

BETTY'S VIRGINIA CHRISTMAS

ing vigorously with Sally Carteret. Betty was besieged with partners, and immediately whirled off with one of them. When the music stopped, she found herself close to Fortescue, near the great fireplace in which the Christmas fire burned. They both spoke cordially and smiling, but as Betty withdrew her hand from Fortescue's grasp, she left in it the little ring. Fortescue was exasperated, as any man would be, by the promptness of this stab, and, while talking gaily with Betty, dropped the ring into the open fire, unseen by any except her. Betty's heart gave a great throb of pain. She loved her little ring, and it seemed to her an insult that Fortescue should destroy it before her eyes.

They danced together, and talked so merrily that no one suspected the gulf which they themselves had dug between them, so great is the folly, the rashness, the headlong pride, of youth. Each had a fierce pride which prevented them from showing their self-inflicted wounds to the world, or making an outcry at that dreadful, gratuitous and unnecessary pain which the young inflict upon themselves. As Betty danced, she thought about the poor princess who had to walk upon burning plough-shares. If she were a real princess, Betty thought, she smiled bravely during her agony.

PRIDE PAYS THE PRICE

The merriment, the dancing, the pretty Christmas observances, that Betty had loved so much, all seemed now to her wearisome and joyless. She longed for the time to come when the ball would be over, and she could be alone, and thought with distaste of the half a dozen parties ahead of her. This was very much increased by the news spread abroad that a ball was to be given at Rosehill on

Christmas Eve. Fortescue invited everybody cordially and pleasantly to his ball, saying he could not hope to do things as picturesquely as they did them, but he would do his best. Everybody had accepted his invitation with alacrity. He had made himself popular in a community where newcomers were usually looked upon askant, and the prospect of Rosehill being once more opened at Christmastime pleased the young people immensely.

BETTY'S VIRGINIA CHRISTMAS

"Of course, Miss Betty, you will come," said Fortescue cordially, his heart hardening against Betty as he spoke.

"Certainly, I will," she answered, with a brilliant smile. "I shall be glad to see Rosehill gay once more."

When the ball was over, in the early hours of the morning, with the earth still wrapped in pitch darkness, and Betty was driving home, a faint moan escaped her lips. It was bad enough to have to meet Fortescue constantly, but to go to Rosehill—— She might, it is true, deceive everybody in the county on a pretense of illness, but she could not deceive Fortescue, the person whom she most wished to deceive. She would go, no matter what it cost her.

The ball at Rosehill was a torturing thing to Betty. By that time, as it is with the wild hearts of youth, she had a settled and burning resentment against Fortescue, which she concealed from the world with pretty smiles and gay words. Fortescue, as he said, could not do things as the county people did, but with well meant generosity he did everything well at his ball so far as money could go. There was a profusion of flowers ordered from Baltimore, along with the conventional supper, totally unlike what the county people had, and a band of music beside which the fiddles of

PRIDE PAYS THE PRICE

Isaac Minkins and Uncle Cesar and the "lap organ" paled. These novelties pleased everybody except Betty, who walked through the rooms where she had spent nineteen years of her short life, and looked around her with a supercilious smile that infuriated Fortescue.

The ball kept up late. Fortescue was an admirable host, and his guests enjoyed themselves. It was quite five o'clock before the last guest had left, and during the night there had been a fall of snow. The lights were out, and Fortescue, in his bedroom, which had once been Betty's, was smoking his last cigar, and cursing the treachery of a woman—of Betty Beverley, who had won his brave and honest heart, and then, through sheer unreason and heartlessness, had cast him off. He threw the stump of his cigar savagely into the fire, and, going to the window which looked toward Holly Lodge, put it up to inhale the cold, clear air. The blackness and darkness had given way to a pale gray, which preceded the dawn, and by the ghostly half-light, he saw from the roof of Holly Lodge a great cloud of black smoke ascend, and little tongues of flame leaping wickedly.

CHAPTER XVII

THE HAND OF DESTINY

WHEN Fortescue saw the thin cloud of smoke curling upward from the roof of Holly Lodge, he sprang up, and, still in his evening clothes and dancing pumps, ran downstairs, ringing bells and shouting aloud as he ran. The servants flocked out half-dressed, and Fortescue, calling to them to follow him and bring buckets with them, sped across the open field to Holly Lodge. Quiet and still was the house in the dawn of the wintry morning, and apparently asleep. The burning roof had not yet awakened the household, as the smoke and flames were borne upward. Fortescue ham-

THE HAND OF DESTINY

mered at the little front door, and, as the flames began to crackle, put his shoulder to the door and burst it in by main force. The Colonel, in his dressing-gown and slippers, was just coming out of his bedroom on the first floor, and at that minute Kettle, struggling into his trousers, rushed into the hall, followed by Aunt Tulip and Uncle Cesar in very sketchy toilettes, Kettle shouting:

"The house is afire, an' Miss Betty, she upsty'ars!"

Fortescue ran up the narrow stair, two steps at a time. As he reached the landing, Betty opened her door. She was dressed as when she left the ball; even the wreath of ivy leaves on her rich hair was undisturbed. It was not necessary to tell her what was the matter. The shouts and cries below and the roaring and crackling of the flames were enough. Fortescue seized her cloak off a chair and threw it around her, then they both fled downstairs. The roof over the little kitchen wing was burning furiously as the heat melted the snow, but a white mantle lay heavily upon the other part of the roof, and it seemed possible to save the house. By that time the servants from Rosehill had come running, and Fortescue, throwing off his coat, climbed upon the roof and organized a bucket brigade. It was hard work to save the little house, but, by the blessing of the snow and every possible device, it seemed as if the fire could be confined to the roof. It no longer raged and roared, but smouldered. On the lawn, Betty and the Colonel and Aunt Tulip, shivering in spite of being well wrapped up, watched the fight made against the fire, and led by Fortescue. Suddenly a cry went up: where was Kettle? Betty ran around the house, calling at the top of her voice:

"Kettle, Kettle, where are you?"

But there was no response. Then Betty, despite the Colonel's efforts to hold her, rushed in the open door of the house, still calling frantically for Kettle. Fortescue saw her, and, swinging himself down from the roof, ran into the house after her. Outside, Colonel Beverley, his hands over his eyes, groaned aloud. Fortescue seized Betty in the little water drenched sitting-room, and, without a word, took her in his arms and carried her out. Betty resisted with all her girl's strength. She was without fear, and naturally venturesome, and she felt that Kettle was being left to his fate, but there was a strange delight, a sudden joy, in being held close to Fortescue's strongly beating heart. Then Fortescue went back to find Kettle. Although the fury of the fire was being subdued, great clouds of smoke were pouring through the

THE HAND OF DESTINY

house, and from the outside could be heard his voice shouting as he went from room to room, "Kettle! Kettle! Where are you?"

But there was no answer.

A vagrant gust of wind fanned the fire once more into flame, and it looked as if the house must go. The shingle roof over Betty's room

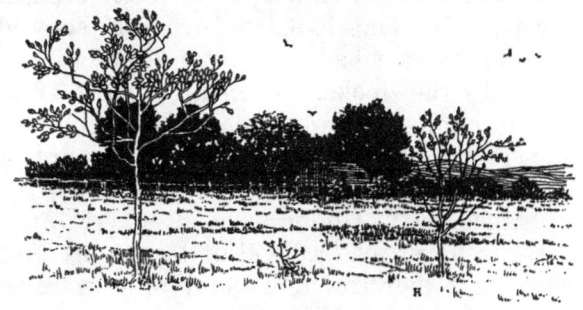

caught fire, and with a great roar and crackling the blaze leaped upward toward the lowering sky. Continually, Fortescue's voice was heard calling for Kettle, as he searched the upper floor, blazing and dense with smoke. Suddenly his voice ceased, and no sound was heard except the roar of the flames and the cries and orders of those who were trying to save the little house. Betty's heart stood still: suppose Fortescue should never come out of the house alive? She turned her head, with its graceful wreath of ivy leaves, away from the blazing house, and could have shrieked aloud in her agony of fear. Then, through the open door of the house, and in the midst of the dense smoke, she saw Fortescue staggering, and carrying a black object in his arms. It was Kettle, frightfully burned, but conscious. In his hands he clutched a little fan which was a part of Betty's outfit for parties. One look at Fortescue showed that he was not badly injured, although half stifled by the smoke. No moan escaped from Kettle, but as Betty ran up he opened his eyes and, looking at her with a pitiful attempt at his usual merry grin, gasped out feebly:

"Miss Betty, I done save yo' party fan."

Betty burst into a flood of tears. At that moment a merciful downpour of rain came from the leaden sky. The roaring of the flames turned to a loud hissing and crackling as clouds of steam mounted upward. It was possible then to take Kettle into the house. The Colonel's room had not been touched either by water or fire, and it was there that they carried Kettle.

"Somebody go for Dr. Markham!" cried Betty.

A dozen willing feet ran to the stable, and a dozen willing hands hitched up old Whitey to the rockaway, and Uncle Cesar, climbing into the little carriage, drove off furiously

THE HAND OF DESTINY

to the village two miles away. Meanwhile, Aunt Tulip and Betty applied such simple remedies as they knew to poor Kettle's wounds. The Colonel stood by the boy, saying to him:

"Be a man, Kettle, be a little man. The doctor will soon be here."

Betty, doing all she could to alleviate the little negro's sufferings, was weeping bitterly.

"Doan' you cry, Miss Betty," gasped Kettle. "Why doan' you do like me? I ain' cryin' none. I tried fust for to save ole Marse's fiddle, an' then yo' party things, but I couldn't git nothin' but the fan, the fire bu'n me so hard."

Kettle closed his eyes and knew no more for a time.

The fire was out, and the men from Rosehill climbed down from the roof. Under Fortescue's direction, they made a great fire in the Colonel's fireplace.

Then began the terrible waiting for the doctor to come. When Kettle could know no more whether Betty was sitting by him or not, she turned and saw Fortescue close beside her. The shock, the horror, the nearness of awful disaster, had torn away all reserve between them. As they looked into each other's eyes, they forgot the presence of Aunt Tulip, still working over Kettle, and the Colonel sitting in a chair by the side of the pallet, his gray head bent, and the rare salt tears of age trickling upon his cheeks. Yet Betty and Fortescue spoke calmly and conventionally.

"How can I ever thank you enough?" said Betty, putting her hand into Fortescue's. "Suppose the boy had died without any one trying to rescue him!"

"I couldn't let the poor little chap die like a rat in a hole," answered Fortescue.

"Perhaps, after all, it was in vain," replied Betty; "but at least you tried to save him."

Fortescue rose and went out. There was still work to be done. The drenched house had to be dried, fires made everywhere, planks found and nailed over the gaping roof.

And so the time passed until the crunching of the wheels upon the ground announced Dr. Markham's arrival. The merciful downpour of rain continued, and, although it was six o'clock in the morning, the murky day was still dark. Dr. Markham walked into the room and made a swift examination of Kettle.

"Will he live?" asked Betty.

"Perhaps so," replied Dr. Markham. "It is a bad case, but he may pull through."

CHAPTER XVIII
"DOAN' YOU CRY, MISS BETTY!"

Some arrangements had to be made immediately for the family at Holly Lodge. It was found that, although the roof of the kitchen was burned off and the roof over Betty's room was badly damaged, three rooms on the lower floor were uninjured, except by water. In the midst of the drenching rain, planks were nailed over the burned part of the roof, and the kitchen and Betty's room were made temporarily habitable. Fortescue promptly invited the whole household over to Rosehill, and to bring Kettle with them where he could be nursed, but this was gratefully declined by the Colonel. It was certain that as soon as their plight was known all the neighbors and friends of the Holly Lodge

BETTY'S VIRGINIA CHRISTMAS

family would offer refuge to them. But at present it was impossible to move Kettle.

When everything possible had been done, Fortescue said good-by, leaving a couple of his servants at Holly Lodge to do what was necessary. Colonel Beverley thanked Fortescue heartily, but that only hastened his departure. When he was gone, Betty went up to her room, from which the open sky was excluded by the planks nailed over the roof, and from which the floods of water had been wiped up and a great fire started. As she looked in her mirror, by the pale light of a cloudy morning, she realized that it was Christmas day. The thought gave her a shock; she had forgotten it until then. She took off her simple evening gown, which was torn and muddy and stained, removed the wreath from her head, and put on the plain black wool gown she wore every day. Then, going downstairs, she reduced things to order as much as possible. Some holly wreaths had been hung in the windows, and the Colonel's portrait decorated with the usual laurel leaves, and the little gifts for Christmas were in a cupboard in the sitting-room. The Colonel was sitting before the great fire, looking so pale and spent that Betty's heart was moved for him. She went up to him, and, kissing him softly, said:

"DOAN' YOU CRY, MISS BETTY!"

"Granddaddy, have you forgotten that this is Christmas morning?"

"Indeed I had, my dear," answered the Colonel. "It has been such a terrible Christmas morning, and that poor little black boy

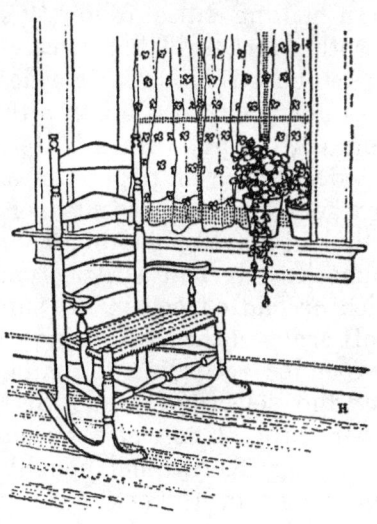

suffers so that it put everything else out of my mind."

Without a word, Betty showed the Colonel the gifts that were meant for Kettle. Aunt Tulip, who was a great knitter, had knitted him four pairs of good wollen socks. Uncle Cesar had bought him, at the village store, a

BETTY'S VIRGINIA CHRISTMAS

top and a bag of marbles, treasures which Kettle had never owned in all his short life. The Colonel had given him a new suit of clothes, and Betty had bought him a pocket-knife. Betty's tears dropped upon these things as she showed them to the Colonel.

"Such a willing little fellow," said the Colonel, with a break in his voice.

In the cupboard also lay Kettle's gifts. Kettle was not equal to writing, although he could read a little, but with infinite labor he had printed on slips of paper the names of those for whom his little presents were meant. Aunt Tulip had a butter paddle, fashioned by Kettle himself. He had a little fund of his own, which he had earned in the summer by selling soft crabs in the little village, and this he had expended according to his best judgment, but the selections made Betty smile through her tears. Knowing the Colonel was fond of reading, Kettle had bought from a travelling salesman a book entitled "The Principles of Hydraulics in Mining." For Uncle Cesar was a yellow cravat with blue spots, and for Betty was his principal gift—a large brass brooch, with a huge imitation emerald in it. Betty put all these things back carefully, weeping the while. "Let us hope, my dear." said the Colonel, "that the little fellow will live to see many Christmas days."

"DOAN' YOU CRY, MISS BETTY!"

In the afternoon Betty relieved Aunt Tulip at Kettle's bedside. Dr. Markham came again, and was secretly surprised to find the boy still living, though unconscious. In spite of the deadening drug that made him unconscious of his pain, Kettle would move about occasionally, muttering:

"I wonder ef ole Marse' fiddle got bu'nd up? I reckon my Chris'mus' stockin' got bu'nd up, too."

A bed was made up for the Colonel in the sitting-room, and Betty was enabled to get a night's sleep by Sally Carteret's insisting on sitting up with Kettle. By that time the neighbors and friends had heard of the calamity at Holly Lodge, and all the day and evening relays of persons had come, bringing everything that could possibly be of use, making every offer of service and each insisting on carrying the whole Holly Lodge family off somewhere else. But this last kindness was gratefully declined, and, accepting such help as they needed, the Colonel and Betty determined to remain at Holly Lodge.

The next morning, Kettle was conscious and in terrible pain, but an occasional sharp cry was the only complaint wrung from him. Whenever Betty would say, her eyes brimming with pitiful tears, "Kettle, I know the pain is dreadful," Kettle would reply stoutly:

BETTY'S VIRGINIA CHRISTMAS

"Naw, 'tain't, Miss Betty. 'Tain't as bad as you think."

For days and nights this went on, but Kettle hung on gallantly to his life, and in the midst of his agony would gasp out:

"Doan' you cry, Miss Betty. This heah pain is a-gittin' better all the time."

At the end of a week Dr. Markham said that Kettle would get well. His burns were very bad, but his face and hands were not disfigured, and although his body would be scarred for life, he might yet be restored to health. The kitchen and Aunt Tulip's room had been repaired, and Kettle was transferred to Aunt Tulip's room, while Uncle Cesar occupied the little cubby-hole where Kettle had slept.

CHAPTER XIX
CALM WEATHER

Gradually the little house at Holly Lodge assumed its usual aspect. The Colonel and Betty were flooded with offers of hospitality and with all sorts of services—those kindly acts which in country communities bridge over catastrophes. Fortescue was gone, having left the second day after Christmas. On that day he had come over to Holly Lodge to say good-by and to offer the resources of Rosehill in any emergency. He had come while Betty was watching Kettle, and although the Colonel urged that he might call her, Fortescue evaded it, and cut his visit short. The Colonel asked him if he himself had suffered any evil effects from the fire. Fortescue replied that his eyes had given him some trouble from the smoke, and that he would use the rest of his leave in going to New York to see an oculist. He supposed it was nothing, and that his eyes would cease to trouble him probably before he got to New York. The Colonel told this to Betty in good faith, but Betty's interpretation was that Fortescue needed an excuse to go away as soon as possible, and gave herself no concern about his eyes. In her heart, however, still burned a deep resentment, and a longing regret for Fortescue. He was so brave—he was so much the soldier—and then Betty would check herself sternly, and try to think of him no more.

As the winter days went by, Kettle grew stronger, and was able to sit up in a little chair by the kitchen fire. Betty spent many hours amusing him, his little round, black face delighted with the simple games she taught him and the stories she told him. His Christmas presents had been given him, and of them all his new pocket-knife was his chief delight. He would sit by the hour before the kitchen fire, whittling industriously, and Aunt Tulip never once complained of the clutter he made. Betty charmed him by occasionally wearing the great green and gilt brooch, and the Colonel religiously read through "The Principles of Hydraulics in Mining." In the

CALM WEATHER

evening, before Aunt Tulip put him to bed, it was Kettle's treat to be helped into the sitting-room and to listen to Betty playing and singing to her harp, or the Colonel playing on his violin. The boy's arms had been frightfully burned, but his hands had escaped. Several times he said to Betty, with a strange look of distress upon his little black face:

"Miss Betty, I want to arsk you sumpin'. I want you to arsk the doctor sumpin'."

"What is it, Kettle?" Betty would inquire.

"I tell you pres'ny," Kettle would reply. But the "pres'ny" did not come for a long time. Then, one day in March, when Kettle was able to walk about and was almost well, he crept up to Betty in the garden, and said to her hesitatingly:

"Miss Betty, what I want you to arsk the doctor is, whether I kin ever play the fiddle agin. I been tryin' to arsk 'im, but somehow I c'yarn' do it."

"Certainly, I will ask the doctor, Kettle," answered Betty cheerfully, "and I am sure you will be able to play the fiddle. Yonder is Doctor Markham's buggy coming down the lane."

Betty met the doctor at the house door. Kettle had slipped away; he evidently had not the courage to stay. Then Betty put her question.

BETTY'S VIRGINIA CHRISTMAS

"Certainly he will be able to play the fiddle," replied Dr. Markham, smiling over his spectacles. "That little fellow is as hard as nails. There isn't one child in a hundred who would have survived such injuries. But he'll be all right."

Betty called Kettle, who reappeared around the corner of the house. He came slouching up, with a faint shadow of his former grin upon his face. Something in Betty's eyes told him that there was good news for him.

"Hello, you young rascal!" cried the doctor jovially. "In another month or two you will be running around here as mischievous as ever, and you will be able to fiddle all right when you get stronger. But you are not to touch the fiddle until I tell you. Do you understand?"

"Yes, sirree," answered Kettle delightedly, his mouth coming wide open. Then, looking from Betty to the doctor, and back again, and shuffling his feet awkwardly, he tried to express some of the gratitude that filled his humble little heart.

"Miss Betty, she treat me white, and so did you, Doc' Markham. I ain' a-gwine ter furgit it."

Dr. Markham went in the house to see the Colonel, who was ailing, and who had been

CALM WEATHER

ailing a good deal that winter. The doctor's cheery smile and pleasant words brightened the Colonel up immensely. When Dr. Markham rose to go, after one of those long and friendly visits of the country doctor which are so comforting, Betty went out with him. Kettle was waiting outside in the spring sunshine. In his hand was a small object, care-

fully wrapped up in white paper. Kettle shuffled up to the doctor as he was getting into his buggy, and said to him, with much stammering and stuttering:

"I—I done heah that folks pays doctors fur comin' to see 'em. I ain' got no money, but I got a mighty nice knife as Miss Betty gimme last Chrismus', and I want you, Doc' Markham, fur to take it. 'Tain't much fur you, but it's all I got, an' I'se mighty glad to give it to you."

BETTY'S VIRGINIA CHRISTMAS

Dr. Markham took the knife, looked at it, and admired it, and put it in his pocket, and then, taking off his hat, shook Kettle's little black hand warmly.

"I thank you, Kettle," he said, "from the bottom of my heart. I never had a fee in my life that meant more than this knife. I shall keep and use it, and whenever I look at it I shall remember an honest little boy, who will grow up to be an honest man."

Kettle's face was shining, as the doctor drove off, and which shone still more when Betty said to him,

"I am glad you gave the doctor your knife, Kettle. You shall have a new one next Christmas, I promise you."

CHAPTER XX
TWILIGHT

THE spring came on apace, but instead of bringing with it the joy of the springtime, an atmosphere of settled sadness seemed to descend upon the little house at Holly Lodge, where a year ago there had been so much of cheerfulness and merriment. The fire had been a severe shock to Colonel Beverley, and all at once the blight of age appeared to be laid upon him. It was the same with Uncle Cesar, and master and man, who had spent nearly seventy years together, both seemed passing into the shadowy path. Oftener than ever the Colonel would send for Uncle Cesar, and the two old men would talk of their youth and of the four years of starvation and marching and fighting during the war, and of times and events long passed, of which they were the sole survivors. When they fiddled together in the evenings, the music was faint; their bow arms were feeble, and their fingering weak. Kettle, now almost recovered, was able to do much of Uncle Cesar's work, and would have done it all if he had been allowed. Even old Whitey suddenly seemed to falter under the burden of years, and had to be coddled as old creatures should be. As for Betty, it was as if in the midst of a spring morning the soft and purple twilight had descended, as if all sounds of life were stilled and the silence of the night were at hand. She could hardly believe herself the same Betty that had laughed and danced and sung so merrily during her short life. There were the same friends, the same generous hospitality, the same kindly attentions from her friends and neighbors as ever, but Betty now kept close to Holly Lodge. She had a very good excuse. The Colonel was growing more and more infirm, and upon Betty's delicate shoulders rested all the responsibilities of three old persons and a child. She was quite equal to it, but she could no longer go to dances and picnics like Sally Carteret and the other girls of her acquaintance. It was true that a way for her to go about was always provided by the kindness of those who remem-

TWILIGHT

bered that Whitey was an old horse, and that Uncle Cesar was an old man. But Betty was rather glad of the excuse to stay at home. She had plenty to keep her occupied all day, but in the soft spring dusk and the moonlit midsummer nights, and the cool autumn twilights she would go into the garden and walk up and down the path bordered by the box hedge. In all that time Fortescue was never absent from her mind. She could see with the eyes of the mind his lithe, military figure, his clear-cut, aquiline face, his close-cropped dark head, and could hear his rich, pleasant voice. A painful and humiliating conviction was forcing itself upon Betty's mind; she began to fear that she had played the fool. At heart, she was the soul of good, practical sense, and an act of folly mortified and offended her as it does those who are sound and sane. After a while, she faced the hateful truth that she had acted arrogantly and foolishly, and apparently without heart. Fortescue had been clearly within his rights, and what he had said about providing for the Colonel and everything being made easy by the power of money, instead of being dictatorial and purse-proud, as Betty had thought, was really generous and provident. To lose perfect happiness by accident or the fault of another is hard enough, but to lose it by one's own folly and rashness was heartbreaking to Betty's frank soul and candid temperament.

"But, after all," thought Betty, when in these twilight walks she glanced toward the pile of Rosehill, mute and dark and uninhabited, "it could not have been. How is it possible that I, Betty Beverley, should ever be the mistress of Rosehill, and have Grandfather with me and be the wife of Fortescue? No, it was too much. The gods are none too generous. I had a treasure in the hollow of my hand, and I threw it away. I shall not have it again."

A subtle change came over Betty's look and manner. She was as brave as ever, but instead of the daring light in her eyes and the joyous laughter on her lips, were the calm courage of endurance and a softness and gentleness greater than she had ever before known. She spent every hour that was possible with the Colonel, sitting by him with her sewing—for Betty did all her own sewing—or reading to him, or playing and singing to him; and to all in the little house, from the Colonel down to little black Kettle, Betty was their light and strength, their guardian angel. Life had turned its stern face upon her, and Betty was learning bravely and quietly the meaning of that sternness.

CHAPTER XXI
RECOMPENCE

THE summer slipped into the autumn, and the gold and brown and crimson October days, with twilight skies of amethyst and pearl, were at hand. Betty's hours were very full. The Colonel was growing daily more feeble, but his indomitable eyes reflected an unquenchable spirit. Only, he was gentler, tenderer, graver. As the year grew old, and the swallows flew southward, and the cry of the wild geese clanged in the blue air, a note of sadness seemed brooding upon the world. Betty was a softer, quieter Betty than she had ever been, and there was a poignant sweetness in her smile and in her eyes, which sometimes held unshed tears. But it was ever a brave Betty. Her smiles were for the Colonel, and the faithful servants, and poor little Kettle.

Her tears were for the few solitary hours she could command. These hours were when she lay in her little white bed at night, wakeful, and a scant half-hour at twilight, when she

could walk up and down the garden path, by the box hedge. And her thoughts were all of Fortescue, and her heart, poor prisoner that it was, beat against the bars of fate and uttered its mournful and passionate cry.

And so the autumn passed slowly.

One afternoon in late October, Betty, hap-

RECOMPENCE

pening to glance through her window toward Rosehill, saw the shutters thrown wide, and the blue smoke curling out of the chimneys. She started and trembled; it was as if a finger had been laid upon an exposed nerve, and she said to herself:

"I will not let anything that happens at Rosehill affect me. I will not let myself dream or wish," a thing easier said than done.

She slipped downstairs and into the garden, and began the steady walk up and down by the box hedge; this walk was sometimes the only fresh air she could get during the day. The afternoon was mild, and some hardy crysanthemums, their bold faces flaunting in the autumn air, sent forth a pungent perfume. Whenever Betty walked in that spot, she could live over again the few happy hours of her love. This afternoon, the sight of Rosehill occupied, and the possibility that Fortescue might be there, agitated her. As she walked along in the red light of the declining day, she glanced up and saw Fortescue coming along the garden path toward her. There was something different in his aspect and carriage from what there had been, so Betty's quick and far-seeing glance showed her at once. She stood still, while her heart beat wildly and the ever-ready blood poured into her pale cheeks.

When Fortescue reached her, he held out his hand without a word, and Betty put hers into it. For a moment they stood in agitated silence. The woman, naturally, recovered herself first.

"I had not heard that you were at Rosehill," she said. "I only noticed just now smoke coming out of the chimneys."

"Yes, I arrived this morning," answered Fortescue quietly, "to stay some time."

"Then," said Betty, "you have a long leave."

"I have an indefinite leave," replied Fortescue.

Betty glanced at him in silence and surprise. They were then pacing slowly up and

RECOMPENCE

down the walk in the light of the scarlet and gold sunset. She saw that Fortescue was thin and pale, and that there were strange marks under his eyes.

"Have you been ill?" she asked, the words coming involuntarily.

"Not exactly," replied Fortescue, and stopped.

Betty's eyes again sought Fortescue's. There was evidently something the matter.

"Have your eyes been troubling you?" she said.

"Yes," replied Fortescue.

He seemed disinclined to give any particulars.

"I remember," said Betty, after a pause, and a thread of light stealing into her mind, "that after the fire, when you came over the next day, my grandfather told me that the smoke had affected your eyes. Did it turn out to be anything serious?"

"Rather."

"And is that why you have an indefinite leave?"

Betty was determined to wring the truth out of Fortescue, and at last succeeded.

"Yes," he replied; "the smoke affected my eyes very strangely. I went to New York, and saw the best oculists there, and they told me my eyes would probably recover, and did a variety of things for me, but nothing seemed to do me any good. Then I got leave and went to Paris and Vienna, with no better result. All the doctors have agreed that to live a quiet country life, free from excitement, was

my best chance. Of course I had to get sick leave, but I would not ask to be retired. I shall fight my retirement as long as I can. I want to be back in active service."

"Of course," answered Betty promptly, her eyes plenteous with pity. "It is a terrible thing to be retired at your age."

There was a pause, and they continued mechanically to pace slowly up and down the garden path in the dying glow of the October afternoon. Presently Fortescue spoke:

RECOMPENCE

"I don't know whether I should have come here or not. But it was so lonely at Rosehill —I can't read, you know—and you said we were to be friends."

Betty, who could usually control her tears marvellously, suddenly felt them dropping upon her cheeks. They came quickly in a flood and with gasping little sobs. It was through her that Fortescue was menaced with this calamity, that this tragic closing of his soldier's life had come, perhaps never to be reopened. Her heart was so wrung with this thought, she did not know that she was weeping, but Fortescue knew it. He felt she had injured him and even insulted him by her conduct, and he had once thought she had no heart, but now a strange and quick conviction came to him that Betty was very far from being a heartless coquette. And with it came a sudden illumination concerning himself. He had been very hasty, very dictatorial. After all, their quarrel had not been about a trifle, but about what was to become of Colonel Beverley, a serious matter for them to consider, and Betty had shown more unselfishness than he. Fortescue put some of this in broken words. He took out his handkerchief, and, with his arm around Betty, wiped away the tears that were streaming down her cheeks, and Betty, the haughty, the arrogant, the resolute Betty, laid her head on Fortescue's shoulder, and they asked forgiveness of each other, like two children that have quarrelled. But they were not children: their hearts were strong, and each knew its mate. A half-hour went by; neither Betty nor Fortescue could have told what passed, except that there were clinging kisses, and whispered pleas for forgiveness, and tender promises. They were so quiet and low-voiced that the blue pigeons which nested in the pigeon-house close by the hedge fluttered around them, looking at them, and making little cooing sounds as they stopped close to them on the brown earth. At last the tension of emotion subsided a little, and Betty made Fortescue tell her all the details of his trouble. His case was peculiar. There was not much obvious injury to his eyes, so the doctors said, only he could not see very well. But that was enough. He hoped that in a year or two, perhaps, with country air and rest and quiet, a cure might be worked. Betty, with all her old confidence, and smiling bravely, declared he could get well, he should get well, he must get well.

They stayed out until the sunset glow was past and the purple dusk had come. Then it was Betty who sent Fortescue home.

"I can't ask you to stay to supper," she

RECOMPENCE

said, "because I want first to tell Grandfather that we have made up. Haven't we made up?"

Fortescue's answer was a true lover's answer.

"We have made up," he said, "and as you know right from wrong better than I do, I mean to do what you think best, Betty, if we have to be engaged for thirty-four years, until I shall be retired, even if I get my eyesight back."

"Very well," answered Betty, with a wicked smile. "Let us see how long you will remain in that virtuous frame of mind."

CHAPTER XXII
GLORIA

While Fortescue was walking across the brown stubble of the fields to Rosehill, Betty, in the firelit sitting-room, was telling the Colonel all about it.

"And you must not worry, Grandfather, about my leaving you," she said, "because Jack has said that he will leave all that to me, and we can find a way, depend upon it."

The Colonel thought that he knew a way, a very easy and good way, by which most problems are finally solved, but he did not speak of this to Betty. He only said:

"Whatever you do, my dear, will make me satisfied."

The next morning Fortescue appeared, and looked much more like his old cheerful self than he had the day before. Betty blushed up to her eyes when Fortescue said smiling, to the Colonel:

"Well, Colonel, I may as well make a clean breast of it. I have come this morning to ask you——"

At this, Betty suddenly dropped her needlework and scurried frantically out of the room.

Fortescue and the Colonel talked a long time together.

"I surmise what your disagreement and my granddaughter's was about," said the Colonel. "I think you both did me an injustice in supposing that I would stand in the way of the child's happiness."

Then Fortescue told about his trouble with his eyes, and his chances of remaining in the army, and all the details with which the Colonel was so familiar and so sympathetic.

It was quite twelve o'clock before Betty and her lover had their next walk up and down the garden path behind the tall box hedge.

Fortescue's arrival had very much puzzled Kettle, and he asked Aunt Tulip what it meant.

"Huh!" sniffed Aunt Tulip. "It means that Mr. Fortescue is jes' dead stuck on Miss Betty, an' Miss Betty, she kinder got a shine fur Mr. Fortescue."

Kettle determined to satisfy himself, and, watching his chance, when Betty had returned

BETTY'S VIRGINIA CHRISTMAS

to the Colonel in the sitting-room, marched in and planting himself before Betty, asked anxiously:

"Miss Betty, is Mr. Fortescue dead stuck on you, an' is you got a kinder shine fur Mr. Fortescue?"

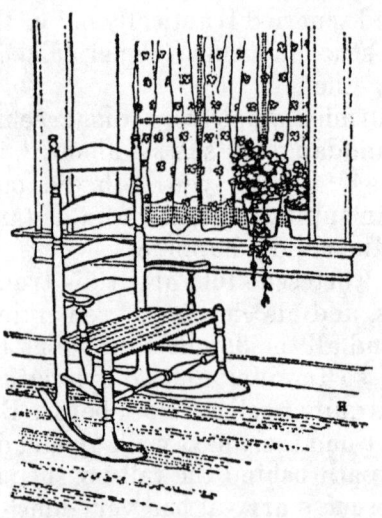

"What do you mean, you impudent boy?" screamed Betty, red and furious, while the Colonel laughed. "How dare you ask such things? I have a great mind to give you a good slap."

"Hi, Miss Betty, Aunt Tulip, she told me so," replied Kettle, deeply injured. "An' I jes' thought I'd arsk you."

GLORIA

Betty could not help laughing, and when Fortescue came for his afternoon visit—for two visits a day were the least he could get along with, so he swore—Betty told him of Kettle's iniquity. Instead of denouncing Kettle, Fortescue laughed uproariously, and, calling the boy out of the kitchen, where he was peeling potatoes for Aunt Tulip, handed him what Kettle described as "a whole round silver dollar," and said, still laughing:

"Kettle, I am dead stuck on Miss Betty, and she has got a kind of a shine for me."

"There, now, Miss Betty," said the aggrieved Kettle. "An' you was a-gwine ter slap me fur axin' you!"

After a week or two, Fortescue mustered up courage to ask the Colonel, since he had said that he would not stand in the way of Betty's happiness, if Betty and himself could be married, and, if so, would the Colonel come to Rosehill to live for the present. The Colonel shook his head.

"No," he said. "Holly Lodge and Cesar and Aunt Tulip and this little black Kettle will see me out my time. It is a part of a true philosophy to take short views of life. You are at Rosehill for another year, anyhow, and I shall remain at Holly Lodge. You and Betty will come over to see me occasionally, I dare say."

BETTY'S VIRGINIA CHRISTMAS

Armed with this information, Fortescue went to Betty, and promptly repudiated his promise to wait until Betty was ready before he mentioned marriage.

On a bright December day, mild for the season, Betty and Fortescue were married

in the old Colonial church. Betty, who loved show, insisted that there should be a real military wedding, and so from the great fortress forty miles away came a dozen dashing young officers. There was a great train of bridesmaids, Sally Carteret leading them in beauty as well as precedence. Never had the old church seen such a blaze of gold lace and glittering epaulets and gilt sword-hilts and splendid chapeaux. Everybody in the county came to Betty's wedding, and waited breathlessly for the entrance of the bridal party. Fortescue, with his best man, both in gorgeous new full-dress uniforms, were waiting smiling in the chancel. Before the bridal train entered, came Uncle Cesar and Aunt Tulip, Uncle Cesar in a new suit of clothes and carrying in his hand a superannuated silk hat of the Colonel's. Aunt Tulip wore a large red and green plaid gown and a black hat with pink roses, and both wore large wedding favors of white satin. Behind them, with great solemnity, marched Kettle. He was arrayed in a Little Lord Fauntleroy suit, made by Aunt Tulip with the aid of a paper pattern, out of an old green riding habit of Betty's. A large collar of cotton lace adorned Kettle's shoulders, and he, too, wore a wedding favor as large as a cabbage, with ends that hung below his knees. In dignity and importance, Kettle considered that he ranked next the bride, and enjoyed hugely being the cynosure of all eyes as he strutted up the aisle. Then came the dozen stalwart young officers in splendid uniforms, and, after them, the rosebud garden of girls in fluttering gauzes and chiffons. When they had all reached the chancel, the officers drew their swords and made an archway of the shining blue blades over the heads of the Colonel, and Betty in her bridal veil. Never was there a more smiling bride in the old church. Fortescue shouted his responses in what Betty called his "parade ground voice," while Betty's answers, though soft, were clear.

The wedding party went back to Holly Lodge, which was too cramped to entertain more than a small party. There was punch in the old Lowestoft punch-bowl, and, according to tradition, the bride's cake was cut with the groom's sword. Fortescue's brothers, fine young fellows, were present, and also his father, who, Betty readily agreed, was, as Fortescue described him, "the finest old dad in the world."

When the time came for the bride and bridegroom to leave for the steamboat landing, a handsome carriage and pair, one of the gifts of Fortescue's father to Betty, drove up, and as the bridal pair passed out, Uncle Cesar and Kettle, standing on each side of the doorway, played on their fiddles the old air which the bands played in the London streets for Queen Victoria's wedding procession, "Come, Haste to the Wedding." The Colonel, in his feeble old baritone, sang:

> "Oh, come at our bidding,
> To this merry wedding,
> Come see rural felicity."

There was indeed felicity on the faces of all, especially on that of the Colonel, as the smiling bride gave him her last farewell.

GLORIA

When all was over, and the guests had departed, the Colonel went back into the little sitting-room. There was Betty's harp and Betty's little chair and Betty's geraniums that she tended so diligently, but there was no Betty. The Colonel seated himself in his great chair, and for the first time turned it around so that he could see Rosehill. Yes, everything was just as it should be——

In the twilight a little distressed voice spoke at the Colonel's shoulder, and Kettle, black and miserable, asked:

"Old Marse, what we gwine do 'thout Miss Betty?"

"God only knows," replied the Colonel.

The Colonel had been without Betty only for a couple of weeks when one morning, some days before the bridal pair were expected, Betty and Fortescue appeared on their way from the river-landing. Betty flew at the Colonel and kissed him all over his face, and shook hands rapturously with Uncle Cesar and Kettle, and hugged Aunt Tulip. The sight of her joyous face was enough to make the Colonel happy.

CHAPTER XXIII

SUNSHINE

THEN began the St. Martin's summer of an old man's life. Every day the Colonel saw Betty, and every day Fortescue performed some act of kindness or attention to the old people at Holly Lodge. There was no more skimping and saving for Betty, and in lieu of her one muslin gown for the Christmas festivities, she had a dozen, and a rope of pearls around her neck, and a riding habit from New York, and Birdseye to ride every day. And there was a great Christmas party at Rosehill, the finest that had ever been known there, so Betty privately resolved. Everything was to be done just as in the Christmas times of old, reinforced by all the new and delightful additions now in Betty's power. The Colonel was to come over and spend the night for the first time since he had left Rosehill, as he thought, forever.

It was cold as on the first Christmas Eve that Betty had met Fortescue, but the great house at Rosehill was warm and alight. Betty's first appearance as the chatelaine of Rosehill was admirable, with everything thoroughly well done. The music was furnished by Isaac Minkins and Uncle Cesar and the young gentleman of color with the "lap organ," reinforced by Kettle. To Kettle, his professional début as a fiddler at "Miss Betty's Cris'mus' party" was a solemn and awe inspiring event, and he sawed away without the glimpse of a grin upon his little black face, but in his heart was exultation. The supper was great and enough for five times the number of guests. Apple toddy flowed, and the eggnog was brewed in the Beverley punch-bowl. There were Christmas songs and Christmas dances, and it was broad daylight on the Christmas morning before the ball broke up. The Colonel insisted on sitting it out, and even did a turn in the Virginia reel with Mrs. Lindsay, in spite of his rheumatism.

BETTY'S VIRGINIA CHRISTMAS

When everybody was gone, Fortescue gave the Colonel an arm up the wide staircase to his old room, and Betty was on the other side of him, while Kettle brought up the rear with the Colonel's stick, while Aunt Tulip and Uncle Cesar awaited the procession in the bedroom. Once in the room, the Colonel looked around him in amazement. There was his bed in the corner where it had stood for so many decades, and his shaving table at the same angle, his arm-chair was drawn up to the blazing fire as if it had never left the spot, and over the mantelpiece hung his sword in its old place. The quaint old daguerrotypes were open on the mantelpiece, and everything was just as it had been until three years before. The Colonel, a little pale, dropped into the chair.

"What is the meaning of this?" he asked.

"It means," said Betty, leaning over him in her shimmering evening gown and with diamonds shining in her hair—"it means that you are not to go away any more. Jack sent four men and a cart over to Holly Lodge the minute you left, and all these things were brought up the back stairs, and Aunt Tulip arranged them. And Uncle Cesar is to undress you and put you to bed, and you are to throw the bootjack at him when you get angry, just as you used to do. For Aunt

SUNSHINE

Tulip and Uncle Cesar are coming here to live, too, and Kettle is to be your aide-de-camp, and Holly Lodge is to be shut up. It is a horrid little hole, anyhow."

Now, as Betty had sworn and declared and protested many times over upon her honor as a lady and her faith as a Christian that Holly

Lodge was a most delightful little place, the Colonel was much shocked at her moral turpitude, but Betty excused herself by saying:

"Of course it seemed well enough as long as you and I were there together, but it must be a horrid little hole without me."

The Colonel submitted, as the old do, and his submission was very much accelerated by Fortescue saying promptly:

BETTY'S VIRGINIA CHRISTMAS

"Now, Colonel, I am the commanding officer at Rosehill, and you will not be permitted to return to Holly Lodge, except under guard or on your parole."

When the house was quiet, and Uncle Cesar had put the Colonel to bed, as in the days long past, the old soldier lay quiet and wakeful in his high-post bed, watching through the chinks of the shutters the dawning of the bright Christmas day. His heart was at peace.

"It is but for a little while," he said to himself.

But the Colonel was to see one more Christmas, a year later. On that day, Betty's boy, the most beautiful baby ever seen, was to be christened "Beverley Fortescue" for the old Colonel. There was to be no Christmas ball at Rosehill, for the Colonel was past going downstairs, and sat in his great chair awaiting from the Great Commander the order to march. The baby was to be christened in the Colonel's room, and out of the old bowl which served both for eggnogs and for christenings. Fortescue and the Colonel and Uncle Cesar and Aunt Tulip and Kettle thought they never saw so lovely a picture as Betty, with a pale, glorified face, and wearing a long, clinging white gown such as are seen in the pictures of angels, holding her baby in her arms to re-

SUNSHINE

ceive baptism. The baby, beautiful and dark-eyed, looked seriously at the new world about him, and acted with the dignity worthy of his name.

When the ceremony was over, and the old clergyman, who had also baptized Betty when she was a baby, was gone, Betty, holding her boy in her lap, sat by the Colonel. Fortescue, looking proudly at the baby, said, "My son shall be a soldier," and the baby nodded, as much as to say:

"I know what you mean."

Kettle, in convulsions of delight, watched him, while Aunt Tulip, in a nurse's cap and a huge white apron, revelled in her new dignity as the baby's mammy.

"Boy," said the Colonel to Uncle Cesar, "give me my sword."

Uncle Cesar took the sword down from over the mantelpiece, and the Colonel putting the hilt in the baby's hand, said to him:

"I give you this sword. It is all I have to give, but it is much, for the sword means honor, and you must keep your honor virgin, and without rust or decay, like this sword. And it means courage. You must fear no one but God. And truth is a sword, and so you must live and act and speak truthfully. When years have passed and this sword comes into your possession, your mother and father will tell you what I have said. May you never forget it."

The baby grasped the sword firmly with his tiny hand, and his great dark eyes were fixed gravely, as if he understood every word, upon the brave old eyes of the Colonel.

Then the sword was again hung upon the wall, and they all went out of the room, leaving the Colonel to rest, with Uncle Cesar to watch him. For in those last hours, the humble serving-man was close to his "ole Marse." Down in the hall, Fortescue was saying to Betty, her hand in his:

"I have a Christmas gift for you that I haven't yet given you. I see the little dent in the locket around your neck and the place where the chain is mended. I wouldn't tell you until I had tested it, but I have had perfect sight now for several days."

For answer, Betty threw herself in his arms.

"Now," she cried, "you can once more be a soldier!"

Upstairs, the Colonel was talking feebly with Uncle Cesar, his mind sounding the deeps and shallows of memory.

"Boy," he was saying, "did you ever see a more beautiful little fellow than my Betty's son? He looks like Betty's father, the son I gave my country. But it is all over now, eh, boy? No more fighting and marching and starving and freezing in the trenches of life. Everything pleasant and Christmas weather for the rest of the march."

"Yes, suh," answered Uncle Cesar. "We kin be jes' as comfortable at Rosehill as ever we was, suh."

The Colonel's eyes suddenly brightened, and he raised his thin figure in the chair, and his eyes saw into another world.

"Hear the music," he said. "The band plays very well to-day; it is playing a fine march for the dress parade. Give me my sword."

Uncle Cesar reached up and took the sword from where it hung over the mantel, and put

BETTY'S VIRGINIA CHRISTMAS

it gently in the Colonel's wasted hand. With his feeble strength, the old man drew it half out of its scabbard, and looked at it.

"It is bright," he said. "There has never been a stain upon it. Here comes the Commanding Officer. Turn out the guard."

Uncle Cesar, who knew what was at hand, answered reverently:

"Yes, ole Marse. The guard is turnin' out."

Then, raising the sword to the salute, the gallant old Colonel heard the last order to fall in, and met, face to face humbly, but without fear and in perfect peace, the Great Commander.

www.ingramcontent.com/pod-product-compliance
Lightning Source LLC
LaVergne TN
LVHW041615070426
835507LV00008B/250